KICK-UPS, HICCUPS, LOCK-UPS

MICKEY THOMAS

THE AUTOBIOGRAPHY

KICK-UPS, HICCUPS, LOCK-UPS

MICKEY THOMAS

THE AUTOBIOGRAPHY

Century · London

Published by Century 2008

6 8 10 9 7 5

Copyright © Mickey Thomas 2008

Mickey Thomas has asserted his right under the Copyright, Designs
and Patents Act 1988 to be identified as the author of this work

First published in Great Britain in 2008 by
Century
Random House, 20 Vauxhall Bridge Road,
London SW1V 2SA

www.randomhouse.co.uk

Addresses for companies within The Random House Group Limited can be
found at: www.randomhouse.co.uk

The Random House Group Limited Reg. No. 954009

A CIP catalogue record for this book
is available from the British Library

ISBN 9781846055232

The Random House Group Limited supports The Forest Stewardship
Council (FSC), the leading international forest certification organisation.
All our titles that are printed on Greenpeace approved FSC certified paper
carry the FSC logo. Our paper procurement policy can be found at
www.rbooks.co.uk/environment

Mixed Sources
Product group from well-managed
forests and other controlled sources
www.fsc.org Cert no. TT-COC-2139
© 1996 Forest Stewardship Council
FSC

Typeset by SX Composing DTP, Rayleigh, Essex
Printed and bound in Great Britain by
Clays Ltd, St Ives Plc

To my mum, my dad,
my family and absent friends for
supporting me

Acknowledgements

I don't want this to sound like an Oscar-winning speech but I would really like to thank my family. My mum, Maureen, dad, Reginald, my sister Pauline, brothers Kevin and Phillip. My lovely children, Aaron and Jade. My best pal Joey Jones, who has stood by my side through our incredible journey together.

To friends like brothers Sean and Mike Walsh, who looked after me when I hit skid row. They still do today. To Ricky Fryer who has been fantastic to me. A great pal. Ricky supported me personally and financially in the darkest of my days. I gave him a hard time when I had nothing. But he didn't hesitate in giving me a few bob in those bad, bad times. People like that along the way are very important in your life. There are little stages in your life when you think you are in big trouble, and then these wonderful people come along and help in a way I could never repay.

To Debbie Stoll, who's been fantastic to me over the

last few years. And to Wings Restaurant – the best restaurant in Manchester – who have allowed me to use the restaurant over the past few months. And to Ian Jones.

To Nick Davidson, who got me on the radio for Century FM when he was managing director. Nick had a belief in me and gave me a great boost of confidence when I needed it most. Derek Hatton, the former leader of Liverpool council, played a part in getting me on the airwaves, too. And to Tony Thackeray and Jimmy Griffiths from Rochdale, who had a better left foot than me.

Tim Lovejoy at *Soccer AM* shared that belief in me. Tim gave me the opportunity to step up when the ladder had been whipped away from under me. I am indebted to people like him and Nick who I can proudly call friends.

You don't always get the opportunity to say 'thank you' but I do now. There are a lot more who have had a major influence in my life but I can't name them all. They know who they are, so thank you.

Thanks to John Neal who came to my home to get me when I first ran away from Wrexham Football Club in the early stages of my career. And to Dave Sexton, my manager at Manchester United, another big thank you.

Without you all this wouldn't have been possible.

Contents

Foreword by Ryan Giggs

I must have been eight or nine when I remember seeing Mickey Thomas the footballer for the first time. He was racing down the left wing for Manchester United with that long flowing black hair.

He was left footed, skilful and entertaining. What was even better from my point of view was that he was also Welsh. From that day I wanted to aspire to be Mickey Thomas. I wanted to play down the same wing for Manchester United and Wales. Incredibly I managed to do that. Mickey though to this day remains my inspiration for achieving my ambition.

I had pictures of the Manchester United team complete with Mickey, my favourite player, on my bedroom wall as a starry eyed youngster who was desperate to follow in his footsteps.

But what is even better is that I have over the years got to know Mickey as a person. Mickey the bloke is just as colourful and entertaining as Mickey the footballer.

He is a bubbly, infectious character. He is someone who can light up a room with his very presence. Mickey has always offered words of encouragement to me and seems to have taken a special interest in my career. It's probably because like him I have gone on to represent our beloved Wales.

I know that he has given me hours of enjoyment watching him during my younger days. I hope that I have managed to do the same for him.

As a footballer he was always instantly recognisable because of his long hair. Again today you don't have to look twice to know that Mickey is around now that he hasn't got a single hair on his head!

We see a lot of him at Manchester United due to his media work, much of it surrounding the club which he seems to enjoy. As players we enjoy having Mickey around and I know many of the lads have been looking forward to this book.

Some of his tales from the past are legendary and so to have a record of them in print will pass the hours away. Afterall Mickey doesn't do ordinary does he? He had a successful playing career and now he is making a name for himself in the media. The good thing about Mickey is that he doesn't just slag today's players off for the sake of it. He can make poignant observations without being nasty. His sense of humour has never left him. It has given him a distinctive style when it comes to reporting on the games and what goes on around them.

He is pretty well unique in the fact that he has managed to place a smile on people's faces not just because of his fantastic ability on the ball as a player but also as a pundit. Mickey is a jokey, fun person. He is as popular today as he was in his prime as a professional player. He has that common touch, someone who seems to be completely at ease when he is dealing with the public.

Mickey enjoys a good rapport with the present day Manchester United players. We like having him around. He brightens the place up. I know from numerous conversations with him that he would still love to be playing at the highest level. Part of him probably believes he still could because he has kept himself superbly fit. I think these days though Mickey you would be expected to track back more than you did in your day!

I think he should be proud of what he has achieved in the media world because let's be honest not many of his team-mates during some of his wild playing days could have envisaged that sort of career. He has fought back from some desperate times and for that he has earned the respect of many people, some of whom may have thought that his days were numbered. But as I've said Mickey is good at what he does now. He fully merits the advances he has made in the media world through radio and TV work.

I'm certain he will go from strength to strength. From a personal point of view I can only thank you Mickey for inspiring me to become the player I am.

Mickey Thomas, Manchester United (and quite a few other clubs!) and Wales. Ryan Giggs (Manchester United and Wales). Sounds good to me.

Foreword by Mark Hughes

I've been a big fan of Mickey since those glorious days of standing on the terraces to watch him play for Wrexham, my hometown club. Week in, week out, I'd cheer the likes of Mickey and Joey Jones. I was a big fan of Wrexham and watched them from 1974 through the good years, right up until I joined Manchester United as a professional in 1980. Mickey was a big star and when he went to United in 1978, I signed as a schoolboy in the same year.

I loved watching Mickey in action. His style of play was so high-energy, like his personality. He always wanted to be on the ball. Technically he was a better player than people imagined he was. I went to the 1979 FA Cup Final to watch United against Arsenal, and I thought he was the best player by far on the pitch that day for United. I thought he played really well. I was really pleased that a person who had an association with Wrexham was out there starring at Wembley. I took real pride in the fact that Mickey had gone from Wrexham to Manchester United and made such an impact. As a young kid, who had only just signed those schoolboy forms, I wanted to follow in his footsteps.

Mickey was definitely an inspiration to me at that time in my life. I remember so well being an apprentice while he was at United. One day he gave me a lift back home to North Wales – the first and last time for me. Mickey was on his way out of training and I said to him: 'Any chance of a lift, Mickey?' 'Yes, no problem,' he replied. 'I'll take you.' So we get in his car and I'm thinking I'm going to be dropped at my mum's just outside Wrexham . . . But no. Mickey dropped me off at some remote Welsh station that was on his route home to Mochdre. I had to wait on the platform for three hours for a train to get home. So I never asked him for a lift again . . .

Even in the short time I was at Old Trafford with Mickey, I sensed that he was more comfortable with the younger element of the club. I don't think he enjoyed the strong characters in that United first team dressing room. You sensed that he was more at ease with the reserves and the youth team players. He seemed to have more in common with them. You would always find him lurking around the boot room with the lads cleaning boots. 'Are you all right, Mickey?' they would always say.

Mickey had a marvellous career. His ability as a

footballer was never in question. It was handling everything that came with being a football player that Mickey found more difficult to deal with. He was probably at his happiest when he was out on the pitch. He was always happy as long as he was playing.

Mickey made you smile, too, when he'd finished playing. I remember being at Chelsea and he would come down to the training ground with Joey. Mickey was always one who wanted to acquire football kits. I would go and say hello, and he would always ask me for one of my shirts. I had to go back into the dressing room and come back and say: 'Here you are, Mickey, here's some more kit for you.' God knows what he did with all those shirts. It was great to help out, though. You could never take offence with Mickey.

He's a lovely lad who hasn't got a mean bone in his body. And he has to be classed as one of the best Welsh internationals of modern times, just because of his energy and what he gave to Welsh football. The thing with Mickey is that he would always give everything he had. You knew he would always give you that.

He will be remembered fondly. There's a bit of notoriety which follows Mickey around because of circumstances off the field. But that shouldn't cloud his ability as a player and the impact that he made on the teams he was involved in.

Good luck, Mickey.

One

Clang. Clunk. The turn of a heavy key, metal scraping metal. Silence. Darkness. Alone. Frightened.

The sounds and raw emotions from my first night in the notorious Walton Jail in Liverpool will never leave me. My mind never stops flashing back over those fifteen years to the day when I became a prisoner. Mickey Thomas: jail bird, convict, lag.

Scared shitless by horrible screams in those lonely hours; thinking unimaginable thoughts about what was happening in those hell holes all around me.

I was always known as Mickey Thomas the joker. The loveable rogue. Yes, I can laugh off any low in my colourful life. Make fun of adversity.

Not this time. Now I felt abandoned. My freedom taken away. My only glimpse of the outside world – where I had been cheered and jeered as a professional footballer for twenty years – was through a tiny window.

Through the bars I could see the skyline of Liverpool

where, tucked away amid the rows of terraced houses, stood the homes of Everton and Liverpool: Goodison and Anfield, where I had played my football in front of packed houses.

Now, my audience was one: my new cell-mate. I felt deserted. Alone. And, boy, was that scary.

Yet, eighteen months before, such desolation never crossed my mind. I was on one hell of a high after scoring one of my best-ever goals in Wrexham's FA Cup giant-killing of Arsenal in January 1992.

TV replays and photographs of my fabulous free kick were zapped around the world. I was the King of Wales at the ripe old age of thirty-seven. I was big news. But not that big, as it turned out. I managed to reign for just seven days before Her Majesty's police force arrived outside my mum's council house in Colwyn Bay to arrest me on charges of producing counterfeit money.

I was a hero one week, a villain the next. I wanted to go out with a bang against Arsenal but I didn't expect it to be the bang of a cell door.

I remember the day everything changed. It was 3 p.m. on a Sunday afternoon and things were really kicking off in little Colwyn Bay. Looking out of my bedroom window, it was like a scene from *Miami Vice* outside the house. I had never seen so many cops; they were everywhere.

I had no option but to go downstairs to let them in. And, you've guessed it, there was a joke not far behind with good old Mickey Thomas taking the piss.

I opened the door and this copper said, 'Are you Mickey Thomas?' 'Yes,' I replied.

'I'm Detective Roberts,' he said. 'I have come about the forgeries.'

'Come back tomorrow and I will get you loads,' I joked back.

Well, I thought it was funny. He didn't. With that, the cops came in and searched me. Some of them didn't want to. They had been cheering me on from the terraces just a week before. They were my fans.

My mum, Maureen, was naturally upset and I didn't want to make it any more distressing for her so, as they say in the films, I went quietly. But driving to the nick I had a moment of great satisfaction.

One of the detectives in the front seat was a bit arrogant. He asked me if I knew his cousin and I said, 'Oh, yes. I've given her one. I had no trouble taking down her particulars.' The other cops were laughing into their hands. He wasn't amused but it served him right for being cocky.

Anyway, they took me away to Flint police station and locked me up. The next morning a big fat policewoman opened my cell door and said, 'You're being transferred.'

'Have Wrexham sold me already?' I joked.

I didn't get much of a laugh as she replied, 'No, you're going to Wrexham nick for questioning.'

On the way they told me I had been arrested on

charges of producing counterfeit money: of passing fake £10 and £20 notes to apprentices at Wrexham. For the next eighteen months I had all that hanging over me, not knowing that one day I would be playing my football on the inside. But all that's later. I still had a job to do for Wrexham. And my next big game was at West Ham in the FA Cup.

I was captain of the Wrexham team and I and their skipper Julian Dicks went into the referee's room before the game at Upton Park.

The ref told us that he wanted a clean game, blah blah. So I went to shake his hand with a tenner stuck in the palm of my hand. You should have seen his face as he backed away, saying, 'Oh for fuck's sake, Mickey.'

I couldn't stop laughing. Nor could Dicksie. I had fun all day, running out to spot a huge banner in the crowd declaring: *West Ham's Bonds are more dodgy than Mickey Thomas's £10 notes.*

The fans threw fake tenners at me and so I bent down, picked them all up and stuffed them down my shorts. The Hammers fans loved it, even though we drew 2–2. It was the first time in my life they had cheered me instead of giving me dog's abuse because I had once played for Chelsea.

It's fair to say that I didn't take my plight seriously. As the months of legal deliberations rolled on, my barrister kept urging me to plead not guilty.

One of my many court appearances was at Mold Crown Court in North Wales in front of Lord Carlile.

I went to the bank and withdrew £1,000 in £10 notes. I knew I was going to get searched before the case, so when they took me down with these two guards, I was determined to have some fun. I'll never forget the look on their faces when I pulled out this bundle of notes and said, 'Look, don't say anything. This is for you.'

Then I started peeling them off into their hands, which were quickly withdrawn amid looks of complete horror. I did explain they were real ones and it was only a joke. Another prank that fell flat, then. I couldn't stop laughing – and saw the funny side again when I was taken to Warrington Crown Court in July 1993 for sentencing.

Who were my guards that day? You've guessed it. Those two guys from Mold. It was a Friday afternoon and somehow I knew I was going to jail. I'd even brought a T-shirt, jeans and my Wrexham trainers so that I could change out of my suit.

There were TV cameras everywhere, outside the court-room and inside. Plus a scrum of journalists all packed into a tiny room. They soon fell silent when I walked in. You could have heard a pin drop. I remember spotting a pay phone and I went over and picked up the receiver, knowing that every eye was on me.

I turned round to the gawping crowd of press men and asked, 'Has anyone got change for a tenner so I can use the phone?'

There was uproar. It definitely broke the ice and the headline in the *Daily Mirror* the next day was: SOCCER STAR GOES DOWN LAUGHING.

The mood was very different, though, once inside the court. As I've said many times since on the after-dinner speaking circuit: 'I played fifty-one times for my country, over twenty-two years. And my career would have been a lot longer if it hadn't been for someone called Gareth Edwards. He finished my career. He went right over the top. I know what you're thinking: Who did he play for? Well, he wasn't a footballer, he was the judge who sent me to jail.'

Yes, Judge Gareth Edwards is someone I'll never forget. I had glowing character references but here he was spouting all these dreadful things about me. I remember him saying: 'You should have been setting apprentices an example. Instead, because it fitted in with your self-image of a flash and daring adventurer, you betrayed the trust of your employers and you failed in your duty as a distinguished sportsman.'

In My opinion this was a load of old bollocks. He didn't know the first thing about me but I just smiled when he had finished his summing-up because I didn't want him to know how much this was affecting me. I was bloody hurting inside, though.

I had brought two kids up on my own, Aaron and Jade, and was looking after my mother Maureen who was dying of cancer. My factory-worker dad, Reginald, had died six years before and my marriage to my estranged wife Debbie was long wrecked on the rocks.

I had done my bloody best to look after my family. To be a good dad. To take care and provide. I didn't have a bad bone in my body and yet here was this guy with a wig who didn't know me, not being very complimentary about my character. I was given eighteen months, taken down by my two guard mates who made me a brew and offered me custard creams, which I felt like throwing in everyone's faces.

Instead I crammed them in my mouth, which was a wise move: the next food I'd be dished up would un-curl a pig's tail. But feeding my belly was the least of my worries. Oh shit, I was going to Walton Jail in the heart of Scouseland. Not a good place for a former Manchester United star to reside when Mancs were the oh so common enemy. I would not be the most popular prisoner in the world, then.

I was shipped out with the other prisoners in a battered old bus, tatty curtains hiding my face from the cameras. I was handcuffed to another prisoner and bundled aboard for the ninety-minute journey down the M62. And it wasn't anything like a team coach, I can tell you.

When I heard that big steel gate at Walton Jail banging behind me I can admit to being scared witless for the first time in my life. Petrified. I could hardly walk to the grim holding area crammed with another 200 prisoners, where we all queued with open arms to receive our prison garb and blankets.

I remember seeing my mugshot on a battered TV high on the wall during a news bulletin. It was a big story. And I was aware of this huge bloke kicking tin trays and cups around the floor. He was a gorilla of a guy and I wasn't about to invite him home for tea. So I sat quietly on my chair and thought, 'Don't let him see you, Mickey. Be invisible.'

They called out our names and lined us up to get stripped. I was examined in a dark place, literally, and certainly didn't bend down in the shower to pick up my soap.

I was then handed my bedding for the cell and felt a tap on my shoulder. To my horror it was the gorilla: King Bloody Kong. And he didn't look too happy.

'Are you that football player?' he enquired with a menacing stare. I just nodded. To my relief he added, 'If anyone touches you in here I will fucking kill them.'

I found out later he came from Burnley and was in for serious violence or something. No one dared ask him exactly what he'd done. And I wasn't about to be a penfriend. But I was glad of the protection as I was taken off to 'A' Wing and my first taste of life in prison. It was a complete reality check. Don't forget this was 1993 and you still had to piss and shit in a bucket on the cell floor.

I remember looking through that tiny window towards Liverpool and the truth dawned on me for the first time: I was banged up. Denied my freedom for the first time in my life. And Christ, that sound of the door banging shut . . . I lay there thinking, This is it, Mickey.

Then at lights-out I heard those screams that chilled my blood. Who was getting battered? I didn't know. I didn't care. Keep your head down, Mickey. But what if I get battered because of who I am? Knifed by some maniac who would regard me as a trophy.

I had already been asked for my autograph by Scousers who said they wanted to wipe their arse on the scrap paper I had written on. But inside my cell I was safe, although I couldn't overcome a feeling of total devastation. I couldn't sleep: for the first time in my life I had gone to bed at night without a bird for company. There I go again.

This was serious, though, even though I was trying to make light of it. I had to get through the night but I didn't sleep a wink until the door clanged open again in the morning. I will never forget the sight of the 'screw' with Popeye arms standing in the doorway.

'Thomas,' he bellowed, 'you're wanted in the yard for a game of football. They're waiting for you.'

I declined his offer. I had played against some hard men in my time but I wasn't about to face a team of murderers and rapists. No way.

There were some bad lads in there and I was very aware of the environment I was in. It was always in the back of my mind that I would be targeted. It was scary. You can't tell anyone that you are bricking it though. I phoned my mum and lied that I was OK.

I had never been so lonely. I was living through the worst twenty-four hours in my life. I was thirty-eight and it was in the back of my mind that I would never play football again. Never mind that, I thought my life was over. But I never thought of topping myself. I felt degraded but I had two kids at home and my mum. There was so much to live for. I'd get through this. Keep my head down. Stay positive.

Thoughts of my family kept me going. I had run out on football but I could never desert them. I had to be strong, even though my life was shut off. I had lost control of my own destiny. As a footballer, it was always in my own hands, my own two feet. Throughout my career I had always done as I wanted. When that door shut on me I had no control of my life for the first time. I had been taken away. Gone. Gone completely. A lost soul.

So I just stayed in my cell. Didn't touch a scrap of food except for a piece of toast. My head was up my arse. And all I wanted to do was stay on my bed and keep my nose clean. I was happy doing that until I was summoned to see the Governor later on that first day.

I was marched into his room and he asked me for my number. I thought he meant my home phone number and rattled off 01492 ... I couldn't remember my prison number. I still can't. I didn't know what was happening. They knew who I was: Mickey Thomas, footballer. So why were they asking? I wasn't about to crack any more jokes, though.

I was told I was high priority and thank God they wanted to get me out of there as quickly as they could. To get me into an open prison. I wasn't about to argue and two days later I was shipped off to Kirkham.

Two

After the hell of Walton the bus ride to my new penal residence, Kirkham jail, was made in a far better state of mind than the tortured trip immediately after I was sentenced.

When I arrived I was taken to the prison officers' quarter where I was handed my new prison clothes for what would be around a two-month stay. Then I was taken to my cell and immediately I noticed some other prisoners jumping up and looking through my window, trying to catch a glimpse of me.

Obviously news travels fast. Mickey Thomas was in town but I was still anxiously wondering how my arrival would be greeted.

Straight away I noticed a big difference in the atmosphere of Kirkham compared to Walton. There was a completely different feeling. There were no bars on the windows for a start. You weren't cooped together in tiny, stifling cells either. You had a little room to yourself and there was a bit more freedom to walk around.

While I settled down in my cell around twenty other prisoners came in, lads from all over the country. One guy introduced himself as the chef. He told me not to go down for my food, he would bring it to my cell. I certainly wasn't complaining about that offer. I was treated as quite a celebrity, which meant I wasn't as afraid as before. In fact, it seemed a far more relaxed regime than I had experienced at Walton. You were still locked up at night but you could have walked out of the jail if you had wanted – not that it ever crossed my mind because I just wanted to serve my time and get out the proper way.

Immediately I was asked to play for the prison football team and I did end up playing a few games for them.

You were also supposed to work while you were there. It kept you occupied as well as earning you a few quid to take home when your time was eventually up. I was well chuffed with the job I was handed. I was stationed in the gym, dishing out equipment and gear in the weights room, which was to prove pretty handy as I will explain a little later!

The food was a lot better than it had been in Walton and for the first few days I went along with it being delivered to my cell. At least it meant I was spared the tedium of having to queue up. But as my confidence grew I decided to start going to the canteen and picking up my own dinner. I also heeded good advice to make myself available for the prison football team because that proved I wanted to be one of the guys.

Even though I still felt hard done by for actually being in prison I was determined to try and make the best of it. I made a conscious decision to make sure my life behind bars was as enjoyable as possible and to get away with anything I could – a bit like parts of my playing career, I suppose!

Mind, some of the prison football games weren't the best. Certainly nothing like I had been used to in the professional game. One game against a team from outside the area really kicked off big style. Our goalkeeper received some verbals from one of their players and he just lost it. He ran to the side of the pitch and head-butted this guy who had called him something.

That sparked an almighty scrap; everyone was getting battered. Everyone except me, of course. I was determined to keep out of trouble, even on the football pitch. Not surprisingly our goalkeeper was in prison for committing violent crimes. He didn't play again – and I didn't play too many more games either because there was always a chance games were just going to explode into all-out warfare. That wasn't for me.

I did play in a celebrity game, which was organised by my big mate Joey Jones. People like Tim Vincent who was then in *Blue Peter* and Rob McCaffrey from Sky Sports were involved. But the best bit was that Joey and the lads smuggled some drinks, including champagne, into the prison.

Working in the gym I had the perfect place to hide it – in the wooden horse, which you used for vaulting. In fact, all my little 'extras' that had been slipped in were dotted about the gym. The store room had a better stock than Bargain Booze. What I didn't realise at the time was while all this was going on one of the lags was secretly taking pictures and they were eventually flogged to the *News of the World,* leaving me deep in the brown stuff.

But at the time I just took advantage of people's generosity and the lax security at Kirkham.

If life at Kirkham had been cosy in contrast to Walton, moving on to my third prison, Sudbury in Shropshire, proved to be an even bigger breeze – at least until those clandestine pictures surfaced.

The idea was to move me to a 'softer' jail closer to my North Wales home so I would be able to visit my family more often. Open prisons allow you regular home visits. My fellow inmates had told me, 'You've got to get to Sudbury, Mickey. You'll love it.' I put out a few feelers and someone up above did me a favour by recommending I was moved to my new gaffe in Shropshire.

I was driven to Sudbury from Kirkham by a mate who happens to be a policeman. But before we got there we stopped off at a pub for a few pints. While we're knocking back the drink who should walk in but a group of prison wardens from Sudbury. One of them was a

West Brom fan – one of the many clubs I played for – and he recognised me. He startled me at first but when I said, 'look, I'm just having a couple of pints', he said that was all right, no problem.

Next stop Sudbury. I was getting quite familiar with all the usual business when you arrive: exchanging the clothes you are wearing for prison garb. Before they allocated me my cell I was taken to a big room containing around twenty beds, all occupied. They squeezed another bed in and I managed to get some sleep. When I woke up the next morning there's a big guy, a real mean-looking man-mountain staring down at me. He said to me, 'Mickey Thomas, I'm a Manchester United fan from Walsall.'

He was a chef as well. (What's it with chefs? Why were so many of them in bloody prison!) He told me to stay put and he would go and get my breakfast. Top-class service!

Eventually I was given my own room and it was like being in a hotel. I was dead relaxed, I had the top chef in the place looking after me; what more could you want?

And then my whole world was turned upside down again. One Sunday morning my personal chef came into my cell and told me I was in trouble. I was splashed all over the front of the *News of the World* – the biggest selling newspaper in the country. It was all there. All those secretly taken pictures of me drinking champagne and larking around in the last prison, Kirkham.

SOCCER STAR – LIFE OF RILEY read one of the headlines. There were pictures of me playing pool, drinking, chatting on the phone.

It got worse. I was featured on the national television programme *Breakfast with Frost*. They went on and on about how a jailed footballer could be allowed to enjoy this lifestyle while he was supposed to be serving a punishment.

I knew I was in serious trouble. No one in authority was going to allow me to get away with this. It was pay-back time for Mickey Thomas.

Two wardens arrived and escorted me to a meeting with three of the prison governors. I was petrified, fearing that their only course of action would be to send me back to a horrible secure unit: Walton here I come.

They asked me to explain my actions. I don't know where it came from but I just went for it and asked them how they would have coped in my shoes: a well-known footballer in prison with some dangerous types? I told them that I couldn't go around being aloof, not being one of the guys. If I had done that I would have got my head battered. Amazingly, one of the governors said that he felt sorry for me and that they were going to look after me.

They had decided to move me down the road to Foston – a unit housing lifers! Yes, people who had committed horrendous crimes including murder. What a favour!

I must have gone white. I almost crapped myself.

Then the reasoning behind this apparent madness was explained to me, which at least brought some colour back to my cheeks. The idea was that I would be safer in this particular life unit because all of the inmates are seeing out the last bit of lengthy sentences and so they are not going to cause any problems in the last few weeks or months. If they did then they would wreck their chances of ever getting out.

It seemed to make sense to me, so off I went and it was nothing like I had imagined. It was like one big house with 120–125 residents in it. Except these residents were hardened criminals. The individual rooms usually housed six prisoners – and I found myself in one of them.

Watching the telly one night I asked this guy next to me what was he in prison for? He told me that he had 'only' killed his wife. Evidently, he had strangled her with the wire from an iron. 'It was just ten seconds of madness,' he told me.

One thing I was forever grateful for during my spell at Her Majesty's Pleasure was that I had played for so many clubs. What made my stay bearable at Foston was the Governor just happened to be a big fan of Everton – another of my clubs.

The first time he spoke to me he asked whether I could get him a signed Everton shirt. No problem, I told him. Peter Beagrie was his favourite Everton player so I managed to get him some Everton gear, which included an Everton shirt signed by Peter.

A week or so later I was walking around the grounds with some wardens and one of them asked me whether it was true that I had given the Governor a signed Everton shirt. When I admitted it the warden said that the Governor had done the worst thing possible for someone in his position. You weren't allowed to accept gifts from prisoners. 'You've got him by the balls,' he told me.

He added that if I wanted to go home now for a few days the Governor would be powerless to stop me because I had too much on him. So the next day I knocked on the Governor's door and said I wanted to go home for a few days. He replied that I couldn't because I hadn't been in the prison long enough for that privilege to be granted. I brought up the subject of the signed Everton shirt and he immediately replied that I would be allowed to go home for a bit. I had only been in the prison for three weeks and I ended up staying at home for four days. I have no idea whether this was actually down to the gift or not.

Once he asked me whether I was having any problems organising my travelling to and from prison. He asked me whether I had a car at home and when I said yes he suggested that I use that. He even said that I could park it in the wardens' car park when I was in prison.

So that's what I did. And being able to do that allowed me to look after the other prisoners. I would smuggle drink in the boot of my car and hand it out to the rest of the lads. There was brandy, all sorts of things. One day –

it was a bit stupid I know – but I bought a load of drink from the off-licence just down the road from the prison. I loaded it into the car ready to smuggle back into the jail but the guy behind the counter must have recognised me and, unknown to me, he phoned the jail to tell them what was going on. Luckily, it wasn't until the next day that my room was searched – and by that time I had distributed the illegal drink.

In fact, one of the wardens who I was friendly with had taken the call the night before and had delayed any search. That saved my neck.

To be fair, I was living the life of Riley. Every week the friendly officers at the jail would take me for a drink at the pub down the road. One night I was with two officers and we got back to the prison late. I was locked out of my part of the jail – and the wardens didn't have any keys for that area. Instead of being locked in jail I was locked out of it!

'You've got a massive problem here, Mickey,' they said. 'You're on the outside when you should be on the inside at this time of night.'

Quick thinking was called for. I was good at that. The only thing to do was for the officers to fetch a ladder so I could climb back into the prison. They found one from somewhere and here I was, up a ladder, climbing *back* into prison with those two drinking buddies in Her Majesty's uniforms. You couldn't make it up!

Eventually, when I had served my time it was goodbye

to all this. I left the prison at 6 a.m. to avoid any media fuss, cameras, reporters and everything. I was on my way back to a different kind of insanity.

Three

Nine months of porridge was enough and I couldn't get out quick enough when the screws at Foston told me I was to be released one morning. I didn't even go to bed that night; I couldn't wait for that prison door to open. But I was desperate to avoid any media fuss. I wanted to be out before any cameras could arrive to photograph my exit. So, you know all about me and money and I knew it definitely talked in prison . . .

Dawn hadn't broken when he opened the door to my return to the big bad world. I was out of prison, legitimately this time, and on my way back to a different kind of insanity. And there was my good old car parked in the usual spot to whisk me back home to Colwyn Bay.

I drove away without a backwards glance. I had to look forward but I wondered what the future had in store for a footballer who had been jailed for almost a year. I was totally alone and I wanted it to stay that way for at least the three hours it took to drive back to my mum and the kids. I didn't want anyone to talk to me.

Back home there were no yellow ribbons tied around the old oak tree. Don't forget I had been back to Colwyn Bay many, many times on my weeks away from prison, so the sight of my mush was a familiar one. Not that I wanted a coming-out party anyway. The mood I was in I just wanted my own company. I felt comfortable behind my own closed doors. I didn't want to get involved with anyone on the outside apart from my immediate family.

And that's where I stayed for weeks, maybe months, I don't know: inside my own little world, in a self-induced solitary confinement. The only time I left the house was a weekly visit to the probation officer, where I would promise that I wouldn't re-offend, which was quite pathetic.

But I wasn't about to break any rules. I slipped into that routine but the day soon dawned when I realised I had to start earning some money. That warder had got my last few quid and I was bloody broke. I didn't have any way of earning money now I wasn't a footballer. I had come out of prison on such a high but now I found myself on a real downer as the months rolled by. I was on the breadline and I started borrowing money just to survive. But then, naturally, people stopped giving me cash and I was too proud to sign on the dole.

I didn't have a penny to my name and that's when it hit

me. Loads of wealthy pals had sat on my mum's three-piece suite. Surely they could have dropped some coins down the gaps. So armed with the kitchen knife I began ripping up Mum's sofa to find some money. I managed to dig out three quid and it felt like I'd won the lottery. Now at least I could afford to buy a baked potato down at the local greasy spoon. The shame of me, Mickey Thomas, former Manchester United and Chelsea footballer, ripping up the furniture was forgotten in the rush to feed my belly.

It would get much worse. My mum Maureen later died of cancer and I wasn't with my wife Debbie. I'd never felt so alone in my life. I became even more morose. I didn't want to do anything. I didn't want to go out of the house. I had reached my lowest point.

Only my kids, Aaron and Jade, kept me sane, along with my big pal Joey Jones, my sidekick all through my life. But they were still the darkest of days. I remember sitting in the back garden and thinking: I have nothing. Nothing. I don't even own my own house. I used to look up at the sky and watch planes flying past, thinking: I used to be up there. In First Class, sipping champagne. Where's it all gone, Mickey? All that money. All that adulation. A guy who had everything. Fame. Fortune.

All the friends I used to have knocking on my door were gone, except for Joey. Easy going, happy-go-lucky Mickey was on his sodding own. Forgotten. People used to knock at my door for tickets for matches, they would call and ask for signed shirts. Where were they now? No one came knocking any more. I had to get a job, any job, and eventually I got one cleaning cars, with the perk of a free motor for the weekend. That was a bonus.

Then I got another job offer from a guy called Ian Jones (known as Farmer) who felt sorry for me. He ran a big construction company and wanted me to work on the roads, laying tarmac. So the next morning I borrowed a bike and I was off riding to work.

The gang just looked at me: Mickey Thomas in a yellow road worker's jacket on a bike – and not the kind I'd been used to. This guy called Ricky Fryer, who became a good friend of mine, was the foreman and although I was embarrassed, he was great with me. I thank Ian, too, because he saved my life. I would have gone under without his help but I never really got the chance to thank him. I thank him now.

So it was up at 6 a.m. in all kinds of weather and off to lay the tarmac. I had a job. Great. Although in the end I didn't have to do any work. My shovel was redundant. It didn't see much dirt, I can tell you. Ricky told me not to bother with all that digging crap. 'Just turn up,' he said. 'The lads like having you around.' I liked being around, too. I started living again. The black clouds were lifting and a big smile came back to my face when Wrexham granted me a testimonial. Joey was instrumental in that. What a guy.

I spoke to the chairman Pryce Griffiths and in the summer of 1997 – a few months before Mum died – the big game was organised against Wolves. Vinnie Jones had no problem agreeing to play. Nor did Ian Rush – good old Rushie. He helped to attract a crowd of 4,500 which was fantastic.

I knew my new wealth wouldn't last long, though. Straight away I booked a holiday with the kids and my brother Kevin and off we flew to the Canaries. Fantastic. Two weeks away instead of nine months. I spent a bomb and returned to pay back the people I'd borrowed off. There wasn't a lot left.

I was back to square one without a pot to piss in. But slowly things started looking up. I was back in the spotlight after the coverage of the testimonial and a job offer came in from BBC Wales and Manchester United TV. I had made mistakes in my life but it's all about how you correct them. I wasn't a criminal. I was regarded as a lovable rogue and I still am. I had a clean sheet. I had paid all my debts back to everyone, although obviously not to the banks.

And with a few quid in my pocket I got back to playing football at Portmadog, although it wasn't long before I joined Amlych to play for Tommy Charlton, a Manchester United fan. It was the lowest of Welsh leagues but I didn't care. I wanted to play football again and the forty quid he gave me for every game was a welcome addition to my new earnings in the media.

Everyone wanted to kick me, of course. And the dressing rooms were a culture shock after the palatial surroundings of Old Trafford and Stamford Bridge. But to me, a Portakabin in the middle of a farmer's field was paradise.

So there I was at thirty-nine, pulling on football boots – after scraping off the sheep droppings from the pitch. I didn't care. It was a far cry from where I had started out my career at Wrexham but I was in love with the game and in love with life again. Things had come full, dramatic circle from where it all started for young Mickey Thomas.

I was happy . . .

Four

To say I came from humble beginnings is not an understatement. Life in a council house in Mochdre, North Wales, was tough and my dad, Reginald, and mum, Maureen, struggled to make ends meet. But it was a loving household nonetheless. My dad worked hard in the nearby Hotpoint factory and my mum did a bit of cleaning and cooking in the local schools.

They couldn't afford to take us children – me, my brothers Kevin and Phillip and sister Pauline – on any holidays. We just went out for odd days out. Mind you, living near Colwyn Bay meant we had the sea and sand on our doorstep, so what was the point of going to another seaside resort down the coast? If we did venture away, my mum would pack us on to the bus to Shrewsbury because she had a friend there. Or we'd get lifts in friends' cars. We didn't have a car. We didn't even have a garage.

Who cared? We were happy and content with our lot.

I only cared about my football and getting up at five thirty every morning to run to the baker's to get the bread for breakfast. It was a round trip of three to four miles but I ran so fast that I swear the loaf was still warm by the time I got home. I loved running. That's all I ever seemed to do. I used to get up just after dawn every day and off I'd run. I don't know why. It just seemed to be the natural thing to do.

It was running, football, running, football. And in between I found I was quite handy at boxing. That delighted my dad, who had been a bit of a boxer himself back in his Navy days towards the end of the Second World War. He never talked about the war when I was growing up. I don't know if he faced any action. But, knowing him, he would have put himself in charge of dishing out the rum to the other sailors. My dad was just like me, happy go lucky. He didn't give a damn. And he loved his sport.

He had a real belief that I would be a boxer like him one day. As a kid, I did box a lot at schoolboy level. I would probably be about twelve or thirteen at the time. What kind of boxer was I? I can hear you asking. Well, I was mad in the ring. Fast, too. I loved it. My dad got me all the boxing magazines before I'd ever bought a football book. Rocky Marciano was my big hero. Yes, I fancied being another Rocky.

That was my dream in those bouts at school or in the local village hall in Mochdre. Rocky was a big influence on my young life. I wanted to be like him because he never lost. He was a real winner. I won quite a lot of my fights and wasn't a bad prospect. I was a fearless kind of kid and I loved that physical challenge in the ring.

I was always up for a good scrap, and I know my dad was keen for me to follow in his boxing footsteps. I never got into any punch-ups outside the gym. All my frustrations were taken out in the ring. Boxing gave me a real buzz but deep down I always wanted to be a footballer.

My dad didn't have a problem with that. He had a battery of friends who were all football mad. Dave Collier, whose son David played for Shrewsbury and should have gone on to be a better footballer, and Sid Gethers were always around. Another of my dad's mates was Phil Norman, a very successful businessman. Then there was Bill Morris, who was a massive Everton fan and took my dad to all the games.

They were a great group of blokes who always wanted to watch games at any level. My dad used to take me to watch Everton and I got friendly with all his friends' sons. When I eventually joined Wrexham, these guys played a major part in my young life. They were my greatest supporters and I didn't realise how much they believed in me. Every game I played in the Wrexham youth team, or later in the reserves, they would always be there watching me.

I always thought, Bloody hell, they must think

something about me. They must have a lot of belief that I could make it in the big time. And it gave me so much delight when I did and my dad and his mates were able to watch me from the terraces. My dad and the boys didn't miss many games from the moment I joined my first team. I hope I gave them pleasure and pride.

Looking back, they were special times. But, as I've said, my childhood was happy in the warm surroundings of a loving mum and dad. They were both strict with me and taught me from a young age to show respect. We didn't have it on a plate but they both gave me the ingredients to live a good life.

My mum used to put me to bed every night at 6.30 p.m. Can you imagine that in today's world, when kids are glued to the TV or their computer games in their bedrooms? I just accepted it as the norm. And I never gave my mum any lip.

I knew from the stories about my dad boxing in the war that he was good with his hands. If I misbehaved I would get a clip around the ear. I got quite a few of them. When it was time for bed, it was time for bed. Not once did I contemplate jumping out of the window and doing a runner, which I would be famous for later in life.

My mum had a big family: the Irish contingent from Wicklow. I always loved seeing my mum's sisters, Essie and Margaret, and her brother Teddy who was a big Chelsea fan. In fact, I had so many Irish relatives I could have played for the Republic of Ireland instead of Wales.

I had made up my mind, though, to play for the country of my birth, even though half of me is Irish – that's probably the loopy bit.

Mum had about forty relatives who had kissed the Blarney Stone and if the Republic had chased me to play for them the Irish folks back home in Wicklow would have been delighted. I had more credentials than a lot of players called up by the Irish. In those days you could wear the green shirt if you had a Dubliners' record in your collection!

I'm told my mum was a young woman when she made the decision to move to Wales for a better life. She caught the ferry from Dublin to Holyhead and soon after finding work she found my dad. Probably in a pub. My dad liked a good drink of beer.

They married and did a great job of bringing up the four of us. She was a great mum. I had a great dad, too. I don't look back on my childhood with any regrets. My mum was typical Irish. I remember many, many years later when I was playing my football in America I phoned her up once. England had been playing the Republic of Ireland and I said, 'Mum, whatever you do don't tell me the result because I'm going to watch the game later.'

She said, 'Right, Mickey, I won't tell you – but it's a shock result.' That's Irish for you.

Life was fun as a kid in that household. And generally I was well behaved. I definitely wasn't a troublemaker.

I had a heart of gold even as a kid and I wanted to help everyone. That's my nature. I never smashed a neighbour's window or got in trouble with the police. Not then.

There were gangs around then but they weren't like the menacing mobs who hang around on street corners today. I didn't see anyone getting pissed on cheap cans of cider. Or, more to the point, beating a pensioner senseless who had 'dared' to look their way. Back then it was all innocent fun – at least where I came from.

The biggest gang I knew about in those days included my mate Joey. And, wait for it, they were called The Parrots. Why? As Joey always jokes, because they kept repeating themselves. Joey used to come around to my house with about forty other Parrots who probably really got their name because they were all fans of a comic back in the sixties and seventies called *Freddie 'Parrot Face' Davies*.

They were fun days. Summer school holidays seemed to go on for ever. Every day was the same: football. We would play five-a-side games among ourselves; go to football tournaments in the area. Go to the pier at Colwyn Bay where there was an indoor five a side pitch. Fantastic. I loved every minute. I could have stayed out all night but I always got back for my tea. Mum and Dad were strict about that.

I could never, ever repay them for the life they gave me. I can still remember my first ever pay day at

Wrexham as an apprentice. I opened the wage packet and found seven quid inside. I'd struck it rich. But I gave all the cash to my dad so he could get a drink and give the rest to Mum. I always looked after them. I bought them TVs for the house, a washing machine. I gave them as much as I could, leaving myself just enough to pay for my digs and buy food.

I didn't want to spend any of my new-found riches on myself. What was the point of that? I got more pleasure out of giving money to Mum and Dad. Later on in life, with all the money gone, I must admit that I've been struggling financially. But I've never let it get me down.

I've lived with hardship as a constant companion all my life. And I think that's why I'm still around today. Always a survivor with a smile. Ending up with nothing doesn't bother me. I counted myself lucky as a kid. And I'm lucky today to have experienced a wonderful, if not seriously complicated, life.

As a kid, I used to say my prayers every night. I would get down on my knees in my little bedroom and whisper the same thing over and over: 'Please, God, give me a chance.'

I still say my prayers to this day. Every night: 'Give me a chance.' And he has always granted me that. What I've done with the chances he's given me has been my decision. The road I've taken has only had one driver.

But, despite my many wrong turns – and I suppose wrong decisions – that great midfield schemer in the sky has never deserted me over all these years of incredible highs and depressing lows.

I thank God for the life he gave me.

Five

At school I was a real thickie – completely unintelligent, barely able to write my name.

But that didn't stop me when I was twelve and thirteen years old sitting on my bedroom floor for hours and hours painstakingly poring over a dictionary in order to write letters to football clubs asking for a trial, but more of that later.

Back at St Joseph's Primary School I wasn't even able to take the 11-plus exam, which determined your senior school. I doubt whether I could have read the questions properly, let alone try to answer them! So it was off to Pendorlan secondary school. I remember my first day: we were all standing in the playground waiting to be allocated our classes. I was one of twenty-six left waiting to learn our fate. We were all in front of a magnificent building. Were we destined to be housed in opulent surroundings? A voice quickly shattered those illusions: 'Right, the rest of you, off you go over there.'

Immediately our eyes focused on a caravan-style structure. I thought, Here we go – this is especially for the dopey ones!

I'm not embarrassed to admit that I was a hopeless case when it came to education. I wasn't a naughty kid, although I did get into trouble for going AWOL from classes to go and kick a ball around – the start of my many disappearing acts later in life. Actually, I was given a desk by myself because I was really useless and they didn't want me to influence anyone else.

But when the bell rang and we were in the schoolyard, now that was a completely different story. There no one would leave me alone, they all wanted to be my mate. They all wanted me to be on their side. When it came to playing football I was top of the class. No one could get the ball off me. Yeah, they might have taken the piss out of me during lessons, asking me what one and one made and all that, but with a football at my feet I called the tune. Even the sixth-formers, who were obviously a lot older than me, wanted me with them. I got into the school team pretty well straight away.

The PE teacher, Richard Dodd, was a real influence on me. He seemed to love me for my football skills. He told me that I was going to be a footballer and that he would get me trials with professional clubs. He convinced me that I had everything that was needed to make football my living.

So while my general education got nowhere my

football education accelerated at a great pace. It did, though, see me having to face the headmaster a few times after going missing during lessons. For instance, if it was woodwork I would slink off and head for the football field to kick a ball. Suddenly the tannoy would blare out, 'Mickey Thomas report to the headmaster.'

He would ask me why hadn't I been to the woodwork lesson. I would tell him straight that I had been playing football instead. He was great, like the PE master: he would tell me that I was going to be a footballer and he wouldn't punish me. They knew I was a non-starter academically. Even the careers officer who visited the school and recommended that I could go into carpet-fitting added with a little sarcasm on the report he wrote, 'Unless, of course, Mickey becomes a professional footballer!'

Away from school, life couldn't get any better. My mum Maureen was great. Boy did she look after me. And I really looked up to my dad Reginald. I'll never forget his advice when I was growing up: 'Show everyone respect,' he'd say. 'Give everything 110 per cent. If you feel you have then hold your head up high.'

My sister Pauline, who played for North Wales at netball, was always there for me. So were my fellow footballing brothers Kevin and Phillip, who had trials for West Ham.

I grew up fast, largely through playing for a youth side, Llandudno Junction, even though I was still a young teenager. A fantastic bloke called Bob Lloyd would pick up me and my next-door neighbour Pete Jones every weekend in a red van and take us from our little village of Mochdre to the games. Bob really helped me on the way to becoming a professional footballer.

I did all right and I was soon playing for the local factory side, Quinton Hazell. Again, everyone was much older then me but it didn't bother anyone. I played alongside hard guys. One of them had real street cred. We were told he was a gangster and a minder. I was quick to make friends with him.

They were all good lads and even bought me my first real pair of boots, so they must have been pleased with my contribution. They were the cloggers who certainly looked after me, giving me all the room I needed to show my skills on the ball. I was desperate to be noticed and that wasn't long coming. It was my PE teacher Richard Dodd who made the breakthrough: he managed to get Leeds United to take a look at me.

I had never been away from home before when my dad put me on the train at Colwyn Bay station at the age of fourteen. I was off to Elland Road.

The problem was I was picked to play on the right side of midfield and, as everyone knows now, I couldn't use my right foot; I owe my career to the trusty left peg. Big Jack Charlton, one of the Leeds and England stars of the time, was watching the trial. I even managed to score but I was still taken off at half-time. I was told that I had done well, even though I hadn't used my right foot once. I quickly replied that I had wanted to prove to them that I had a left foot as well!

I never heard from Leeds again – well, not until I ended up playing for them much later in my career. I was upset when they didn't invite me back. It was a real downer for a time, that was until a Wrexham scout, Evan Williams, came calling.

In the meantime, most nights I was burning the midnight oil writing those letters to clubs, pleading for a trial. Each letter would take ages because, as I've told you, I could hardly write my own name. And if I wasn't writing letters to clubs all over the country, like Aston Villa and Southampton, I was getting up at 4 a.m. to kick a ball on Colwyn Bay beach.

I was football daft. All my spare money would go on buying football magazines. It was football, football, football.

No one taught me any skills. I learned most of them once the sun had come up on the beach kicking a ball for hours and hours. It proved worthwhile when Wrexham gave me an opportunity to fulfil my dream of becoming a professional footballer.

Evan Williams was true to his word and he did get me a trial with Wrexham. It was at Llandudno. I was fifteen and selected to play on the right wing. At left-back was my big mate at the time – and still is to this day – Joey Jones. I scored a hat trick but the only thing that Evan said was that I didn't seem to have a right foot. I told him I didn't need one with a left foot like mine!

Joey and I had already played in a number of sides together and to our delight we were both told we would become apprentices with Wrexham. So one Monday morning off we went, Joey and I, by train to Wrexham to start a new adventure. Neither of us had ever been away from home and it was hard being miles from our families for days on end.

John Neal was the manager and he was to become a father figure for me. But I tell you it was a hard apprenticeship, nothing like it is in today's game, where young players are mollycoddled, with everything at their beck and call. In those days you were plonked into digs and part of your work entailed sweeping out the stand and terraces of the ground, helping with the pitch, cleaning boots. You weren't spared anything. Most of your £7 a week went on paying for the digs and the train fare. In fact, Joey and I would thumb lifts home and back again to try and save some money. Cash wasn't in plentiful supply and Joey and myself weren't the best of dressers. We both had one going-out shirt and a couple of pairs of jeans. Hardly gear that would have got us in *OK!* magazine as footballing fashion stars of the future.

Joey and I soon became known as the terrible twins. We would hide from the groundsman to avoid doing some of those mundane apprentice jobs. We were a couple of football-mad scallywags from council estates. Rough and ready for any scam that was going.

Our careers were to run in tandom at Wrexham, Chelsea and Wales. We met when we were fourteen and Joey reminds me to this day of our first meeting when we both got picked for Clywd and Conwy under-15s. I was waiting at the stop to be picked up in Colwyn Bay by the schools' bus and Joey was already in his seat.

Joey remembers: 'I saw this lad standing at the bus stop, holding a pair of football boots. He had a school tie on. Red and grey it was and in every grey section Mickey had written "Everton FC" in biro. Right then, I thought, this lad will do for me.'

We became close friends at that moment for the rest of our lives. Sharing so much fun, laughter – and many, many tears. We were brothers. No one could ever divide us. No one could get the better of us. I was as daft as a brush. Joey was a wild boy, too, but he was just that little bit more sensible than me.

Not when it came to one of our pranks, though. We would in our idle moments – and there were many of them – have races up to the top of the floodlights to see who could be the first up the pylons. I regularly won and succeeded in putting a few grey hairs on John Neal's head when he saw two of his young stars shinning up the metal structures which towered over the Racecourse Ground.

It makes me ill now just thinking about it.

At our digs together we were a nightmare. We just couldn't settle and eventually we were split up and put in separate digs.

But the football side of things went well, mainly because of John Neal. He always had great faith in me. He would stand on the side of the pitch encouraging me in games. 'Go on, Michael son,' he would yell.

I was super fit, dedicated to football and could knock the ball around for fun. He seemed to love me. It was a hard way to learn your profession – it's a damn sight easier now. But it was well worth it. I progressed through the teams and made my first-team debut at the age of seventeen.

John called me into the squad for our Division Three game away to Bournemouth. I made it to the substitutes bench and was sent on when we were trailing 3–0. Ted McDougall and Phil Boyer were up front for Bournemouth and running riot.

Anyway, with my first touch I put the ball through Mel Machin's legs. He told me that if I did that again then he would break my bloody leg. As it was Boxing Day, I told him that wasn't very nice for Christmas time. He replied that he 'couldn't give a fuck'. And that he would still break my leg!

A few minutes later I smashed in a great shot but their goalkeeper, Fred Davies, managed to save it. Although we ended up losing 4–0, I did earn some good reviews for my performance in the papers.

A couple of months later John called me into his office and signed me as a professional. What a moment. My dream had come true. But that tendency to self-destruct, which has followed me throughout my life, wasn't far away from the surface.

My first wage as a professional was £25 a week, which wasn't bad for someone who had never had any money. The fans loved me; my mate Joey was in the side as well. What more could I wish for?

But the opening day of one season we beat Walsall 2–0 and I decided to go missing for the first time as a professional footballer – something everyone would have to get used to in the following years. I can't tell you why to this day, but I just went home – and stayed there for a week. I simply didn't want to go back to play for Wrexham. My family and friends couldn't understand it and my dad, Reginald, told me: 'Don't be stupid, son. Get back there and get your head down.'

It wasn't as easy as that. I was having one of those brainstorms, which have struck me at regular intervals. God knows where they come from.

I had even been Man of the Match for the Walsall game. It wasn't even as if I had come back home for a reason. I barely moved for a week.

Luckily for me and my career John turned up on my doorstep and asked me to go back to Wrexham with him. He told me that I could stay with him and his family – that it would help me. And so I stayed with him for a few months while I tried to sort out my head. It helped me get on with my football and I was soon attracting the attention of other clubs.

Spurs were intent on signing me, for instance. That was mostly down to me scoring two goals in a 3–2 win in the FA Cup against them. I recall Pat Jennings, their top goalkeeper at the time, waiting for me by the tunnel. He said that he hadn't known who I was before the game – but he certainly knew who I was now!

There was speculation about me leaving Wrexham for other clubs all the time but I was happy where I was. I was also playing for Wales and I knew that I owed John a lot. If it hadn't been for him my career would have been destroyed before it really had a chance to take off.

Wrexham came to prominence during this period through some great Cup games. We were really making the headlines. The great Bill Shankly, who had retired from Liverpool, used to come down to Wrexham's Racecourse Ground a lot. He even told me after I had scored against Bristol City in one Cup match that it was the best goal he had ever seen. Bill would talk to me all the time and I even found out that he had wanted to sign me when he was manager of Liverpool. You can't imagine what sort of buzz that gave me.

We were steamrollering teams and giving the big boys the fright of their lives. We played Liverpool in the League Cup at a time when they had just signed Graeme Souness, someone who never took any prisoners. I could hear him in the Liverpool dug-out anytime I went near ordering his new team-mates to 'kick that little Welsh bugger'.

The pinnacle of Wrexham's achievements as a battling Third Division club was reaching the quarter-finals of the European Cup Winners' Cup. Mind, when we were playing the second leg – we ended up being narrowly knocked out – I was lying in hospital wondering whether I was going to end up losing my left leg.

I had suffered a knock in a game and didn't think too much of it at the time, only for the leg to become infected. I remember being in my digs at Wrexham and feeling this great pain. I could hardly move. I banged furiously on the wall to alert a neighbour. The medics were on their way.

There was no messing about and I was rushed to hospital by ambulance. I ended up on a drip and was in there for weeks. I was absolutely petrified because I was told that if the poison didn't go I would have to have my leg amputated – it was that famed left leg as well! It was really touch-and-go for weeks. John came in to see me regularly and even brought the legendary Malcolm Allison with him on one occasion to try to cheer me up. Luckily the medical people won the battle to save my leg but it had been really scary.

Eventually I recovered and I was at Wrexham for another couple of years, helping them in my final season win promotion to Division Two.

It was inevitable that I would leave one day because there had been so many clubs trying to sign me. What happened next changed my life completely, turned me upside down. I was never to be the same Mickey Thomas again after joining Manchester United.

Six

My transfer to Manchester United was big, big news. But looking back now I never, ever realised just what a momentous move that would be for me to go from Little Wrexham to the mighty Manchester United. I was in total awe of everyone and everything. I felt inadequate. Lost. Lonely. Not believing for one moment that I could possibly live up to all the high expectation of the manager Dave Sexton and the United supporters. My legs buckled at the thought of playing at Old Trafford. My mind went numb.

I learned not to express my inner feelings. But you know what they say about the face behind the painted smile. Let me explain. How many can remember me laying claim to being the *first* winker at Manchester United? The fabulous Cristiano Ronaldo was caught out winking after Wayne Rooney was sent off in the 2006 World Cup and that image has been shown countless times across the world.

My wink was broadcast every week for years in the opening credits to Saturday night's *Match of the Day*. It was a cheeky-chappy facial expression which had Tottenham fans bombarding me with hate mail, as Mickey Thomas was branded the first serial diver. And radio's Talk Sport still consider the incident to be the start of the diving disease.

It happened in all innocence, really, in a game against Spurs. I flicked the ball past Glenn Hoddle and I immediately went to ground, winning a free kick. My United team-mate Arthur Albiston came running towards me and I lifted my head from the turf and gave him that wink. I didn't know a camera had caught me in the act.

The wink portrayed me as being happy-go-lucky. Not so much cocky, more a fun-loving guy. Content and secure in my new Old Trafford home. But that picture didn't tell the true story. Not by a long way. Forget the smile, I was a fragile young man who was going through a marriage break-up and feeling so much pressure performing in front of my own fans that I would eventually walk out on the greatest club in the world.

Not many can stand up and admit they were scared shitless about playing for United. It's embarrassing to do so. But I can honestly say that I couldn't handle the pressure of playing in front of the faithful at Old Trafford. I was a Red Devil living in hell.

Going AWOL more times than George Best, refusing to attend training and deliberately missing a flight to the

Far East for a club tour were my worst moments in my United life. But I had no idea so much turmoil awaited me when I joined the club from Wrexham in 1978. God, I remember it well.

Wrexham were doing fantastically well and I was on top of my game, week in week out. There was a lot of talk about the big clubs chasing me. I was twenty-three and saying 'no' to the likes of Tottenham, Aston Villa, Sunderland and Newcastle, who even sent an official to knock on my hotel bedroom door and ask me to play for them before a Wrexham game at St James' Park.

I was as happy as Larry, loving it in my own little Welsh world, when suddenly my life was changed for ever by a phone call one Friday afternoon from a *Sun* journalist called Peter Fitton. His gruff words bellowed down the line: 'Are you Mickey Thomas?' With a hesitation in my voice I replied, 'Yes.' I didn't have a clue who this guy was, but he told me that Manchester United were going to sign me.

I put the phone down, played the following day and we won 3–1. The next morning the phone rang again. The same guy said: 'The deal's on.' It was like some kind of Mafia code. 'You are going to sign for United.'

Again I was left puzzled and went to training as usual on Monday morning, expecting the manager Arfon Griffiths to pull me to one side. He said nothing, just named the team to play against Leicester at Filbert Street on the Wednesday, and I left the training ground with the usual warning about not drinking two days before a game.

No shagging either. Bloody killjoys. They were the rules but I don't do rules and I went out for a few drinks on the Monday night with the daughter of the landlady from my digs. We only nipped down the boozer for a few pints and I got back to the house at almost midnight.

I saw the landlady jumping up and down in the doorway and I knew what was coming. I'd been caught out by the gaffer who was on the phone waiting to speak to me. Arfon just said, 'I don't care where you have been but Manchester United have made a £300,000 bid for you. You're going to go – we need the money.'

The next day I was off to United for a medical, hoping the docs wouldn't smell the beer on my breath. That would have given a great impression at a club where George Best went off the rails through sex, hugs and rock and roll. I passed of course.

I met up once more, though, with the Wrexham boys and was made captain for my last game at Leicester. I scored in the first half. It was a great way to say goodbye and I waved my final farewell to the fans with ten minutes to go. I was in a blur and invited to meet United manager Dave Sexton in the manager's office at Filbert Street.

It was the first time I had met him and he told me, 'You're the type of player we have been after for a long time. What do you want?'

Immediately I replied, 'No, listen, I'm not bothered about money. I just want to be a footballer, Mr Sexton.'

Money was not an issue. I had just been given the opportunity to join the biggest club in the world and I couldn't have given a damn about wages. Looking back, I think he told me they would pay £18,000 into a pension, which I still receive today. Mr Sexton also told me I would get £450 a week – three hundred quid more than I was on at Wrexham.

I was rich beyond my wildest dreams in other ways: joining a club where Bestie, Bobby Charlton and Denis Law had been hailed heroes. I, too, was thrust into the spotlight at a press conference the next lunchtime. Suddenly I realised just how big this club was. Wow.

Did I start to feel insecure? Unsure? In my shell?

I was back at Old Trafford twenty-four hours later to meet my new team-mates, driven to the ground by my landlady's daughter. This time there were no high jinks. Not that I was in the mood anyway. I felt sick to the bottom of my stomach and she had to stop on the motorway to let me throw up on the hard shoulder. I was that nervous, but after a few more sick-stops along the way we arrived at my new home.

It took some getting used to. I didn't have a clue where to go and wandered into the souvenir shop to ask the way to the players' entrance. Luckily, Arthur Albiston came in and showed me the way. In the dressing room Martin Buchan stood up and introduced himself as Manchester

United's captain. Next came handshakes with Joe Jordan, Gordon McQueen, Jimmy Greenhoff, Steve Coppell, Sammy McIlroy. I had arrived.

Later that day, Dave Sexton named the team to travel down to Stamford Bridge to meet Chelsea. I was in. My name alongside Coppell, Jordan and McQueen. And the next thing I knew, we were off to London by train – First Class. I'd only ever travelled in Second Class with Wrexham and I kept myself to myself in the plush carriage.

That night I was roomed with Gary Bailey who was also making his United debut. There was no arsing around that night. This was Manchester United. This was serious. Anyway, I had this big South African guy in the next bed and I couldn't be happier. I couldn't sleep and was up at 6 a.m. much to his annoyance. He would be the first of many United players who refused to room with me because of my dawn habits.

I couldn't eat the pre-match meal of steak and chips. Food was the last thing on my mind before we boarded the team coach for Stamford Bridge. I remember we had a police escort. I was used to that, of course, although normally they were behind me.

I'm not exaggerating when I say there were hundreds of telegrams waiting for me underneath my peg in the dressing room. From a traffic warden in Wrexham, the Houses of Parliament from a Welsh MP and from my mate Joey. That's when I noticed for the first time the big difference between this dressing room and the one I had left behind at Wrexham. A week ago there was laughter and banter. This room was full of tension and immense pressure. I didn't like that.

But a quick trip to the bogs and I was out, down the tunnel, with that famous number-eleven shirt on my back. George Best's number. My mind raced back to film of him playing for United until the referee's first whistle jolted me into reality. I can't remember much about that game, apart from making a goal for Jimmy Greenhoff and we won 1–0. Then it was back on the coach to Euston Station for the train ride home.

My new boss was delighted and he told the press at Stamford Bridge: 'The lad made a smashing debut. He used the ball well. He made a lot of good crosses and he settled in on the wing superbly. He is a confident little fellow and is full of himself.'

My career couldn't have got off to a better start. THOMAS WAS SMASHING – SEXTON blazed the headlines. I was off and running – straight back to my mum's council house, pleased with myself of course, and in time to watch *Match of the Day*. There was little me in a red shirt. Bloody hell, I had dreamed of seeing myself like that as a kid, lying on the floor, my head propped up by my hand, watching United in black and white.

The following week it was my home debut against Tottenham. We won the game 2–0 and I can still hear the Stretford End singing, 'There's only one Mickey Thomas.'

But that's when the doubts first invaded my head. Could I handle all this? I still wish to this day that I could have gone somewhere else instead of joining United. I was like a startled rabbit in the Old Trafford headlights.

I didn't really express myself as much as I would have done somewhere else. I always played well within myself. There was a lot more pressure than I could have ever imagined, especially in front of the home supporters, even though I knew they loved me. Sometimes it was too much to bear. I felt fear: fear of not being the person I was at Wrexham. Gone was the happy-go-lucky lad and I knew he wouldn't come back while I was at United.

I was plagued with nervous tension. I was being strangled by pressure. I was in awe of this massive club and, thinking back now, I just wish I had had someone to support me like Sir Alex Ferguson, who later was to guide youngsters like Ryan Giggs and Paul Scholes. People at the club then thought I could handle anything. I couldn't.

I didn't feel as though I deserved to be a Manchester United player. I was always the first to arrive at training at the Cliff in Salford but I used to go and sit in the reserve team dressing room. I was recognised wherever I went but I wasn't comfortable with my new life in the public eye. I meant a lot to people. Their lives revolved around me and I was in the best team in the world. Mickey Thomas, Manchester United. Mickey Thomas, Wales. You can't get better than that.

There was adulation but I didn't have my own space. I had fans parked outside my house back in Colwyn Bay, peering through the windows. Police stopped me, asking me to sign this and that without getting a ticket. Girls threw themselves at me. People bought me drinks. Restaurants opened to me when they were closed.

It was a different world. I recall Martin Buchan telling me I had to go and open a store in Manchester, along with Manchester City's Asa Hartford. I was only there for half an hour and this guy came up and gave me £500. That was in 1978. So next morning I went straight to the captain, Martin Edwards, and gave him the money.

'No,' he said. 'That's for you for opening the store.'

I couldn't believe it and, of course, I quickly blew the lot. That's the first time the money in my pocket became a problem.

I looked after my family but I bought the nice clothes, flash cars – and turned to drink, especially on a Friday night before every game at Old Trafford. I always downed a couple of bottles of wine just to relax me because I was so wound up. I was playing in front of fifty thousand United fans and I was desperate to please them. In the end, the pressure brought me down and I walked out.

I cut my own throat like I normally do. I'm that type of person. But I left with great memories – and some funny moments. Like the time I flew to Northern Ireland with United great Paddy Crerand to receive their Player of the Year award. We landed at Belfast airport bound for the most bombed hotel in the world, the Europa. I went to get in this car with my wife Debbie – we were together then – and I swear to God it was like a scene from a cartoon where you opened the door and it fell off.

The driver struggled to start this wreck of a car but eventually we were off, only to break down in the middle of nowhere. Remember this was Northern Ireland at the height of the troubles. Suddenly this car stops. There are no markings on it and these two guys jump out with bloody machine-guns.

'Who are you?' one of the gunmen asked the driver.

He nervously replied, 'I've got Mickey Thomas in the back and I'm driving him to Belfast.'

They are then staring at me. 'Mickey Thomas?' they barked into the back. 'Get out of the car. You're coming with us.' I feared the kidnapping of a United star. How much would they get for me? Would I be killed?

I was jarred back to reality when they explained that they were armed soldiers and that we were smack in the middle of bandit country.

'Where are you going?' they said.

'The Europa Hotel,' I spluttered.

'Then get in our car and bring the missus.'

My driver piped up, obviously crapping himself, 'What about me?'

'You don't play for Manchester United,' they shouted and drove off, leaving him in no man's land.

And there were good times, like our FA Cup run in 1979. We went to Maine Road, Manchester, for our semi-final clash with big rivals Liverpool and I played my best game. I got the Man of the Match award and we drew 2–2. We were winning with seconds to go when Alan Hansen equalised.

We came off the pitch dejected. Now we had to go to Goodison Park for the replay and Everton fans sent loads of telegrams and letters begging us to 'beat the Scouse bastards'.

We did and I will never forget that final whistle. I was going to Wembley. It was like a dream and in no time at all I found myself in the line-up on the famous pitch being introduced to Prince Charles.

Martin Buchan told His Royal Highness I was from Wales and he enquired, 'What part of Wales are you from?'

I told him Colwyn Bay and he added, 'Oh yes, I have been there.'

Quick as a flash I asked him, 'You haven't been with my missus, have you?'

Sadly, after the laughter came the tears, with Arsenal beating us 3–2.

*

There was more heartbreak to come back in Manchester, where I was nearing the end of my United life. I began to stay away from training, although the press never found out. United were good to me, despite the problems I caused. My marriage wasn't working out and I had psychological problems I couldn't sort out. I was always picked, though, and we went on a winning run of fourteen games to the end of the season when they sacked Dave Sexton.

The writing was on the wall for me, too. In early summer we were due to go on a tour to Kuala Lumpur and Singapore. We flew down to Heathrow and I got my tickets to get on the next plane to the Far East. Suddenly I decided not to go. I was through with United and couldn't face another season of stomach-churning pressure. I turned to Lou Macari and Joe Jordan and told them I wasn't going. They just laughed and bet me £50 I wouldn't do a runner.

I proved them wrong. I jumped on the shuttle back to Manchester. My luggage went to Kuala Lumpur – and I never got that fifty quid. My fate was almost sealed. Dave Sexton had gone and I thought: I really don't want to be here, now. This is too big a club for me.

Eventually, I got summoned to see the chairman and he said, 'You're the fans' favourite. You've been voted Player of the Year. Do you want more money?'

No, I bloody didn't. I just wanted out. I couldn't take any more. I had turned again to gambling and drinking and I had to get away from Old Trafford to find my sanity once more.

Ron Atkinson eventually took over and he, too, summoned me to his office.

'What's the problem?' he asked.

I answered: 'Gaffer, I don't think I can really express myself here. I'm not doing justice to the club or to myself. I can't handle all this pressure.'

Big Ron told me he wanted me to stay but I knew deep down that was as likely as him missing a sunbed appointment to get that famous orange tan.

It took me half an hour to get home that day and I went to my sister Pauline's house. Almost immediately the phone rang. It was Howard Kendall at Everton. I was about to make the biggest mistake of my life in leaving Manchester United. It was the worst decision I could have ever made. At the time, though, it was a huge relief. A mighty weight off my mind.

For the first time in ages, after all those tortured days, weeks and months, I would be *me*. The return of the real Mickey Thomas, this time in the blue of Everton. I wasn't scared any more.

Seven

The dark clouds of despair that had descended during my final months at Old Trafford slowly began to lift the day I met Howard Kendall at Goodison Park. Here I was joining Everton and escaping the pressure of playing for Manchester United. Little did I know then that my biggest high would be flying off on a private plane to sign for Brighton after a major fall-out with the Everton manager.

I still don't hold any grudges, though. I respect Howard for being the great player he was. A hero for Everton. He certainly didn't have to say much to get me to sign for Everton. I desperately wanted to play for his club. Howard will go down in history as turning the club around and even though he became another ex-boss of mine, I will never slag him off. As far as I'm concerned, he was one of the greatest managers of all time for Everton and I admire him for what he achieved in his time in the game.

I remember clearly that first meeting with Howard when I didn't even touch on the subject of how much money he was going to pay me. I wasn't concerned about that. All I wanted was to play football, and play without the pressure of wearing the red of Manchester United. It wasn't a great deal in the end, but I sacrificed so much to get away from Old Trafford.

Now, I felt at peace, at ease. I could relax and look forward to playing my football on a new stage. So there was no hesitation in signing the contract. My signature hadn't dried before I was bounding out of Howard's office and planning for the future. I went straight into pre-season training and my first game for Everton was at home against Birmingham City. We won 3–1. I didn't score but the game couldn't have gone any better.

That morning I had gone to pick up my tickets from the office at Goodison and I heard this fan say, 'There's Mickey Thomas over there.'

His mate said, 'He's only small.'

And the first guy answered, 'I don't give a shit how small he is as long as he can kick a ball for our club.'

So it was great a few hours later to completely answer any doubts in those Everton fans' minds.

I got the Man of the Match award and couldn't have got my Goodison career off to a better start. More to the point, I was enjoying my football again and, in fact, played thirteen games out of thirteen for my new club. Times were good. Kendall, then player-manager, had been busy in the transfer market and brought in Neville Southall, Alan Ainscow, Jim Arnold, Alan Biley, Mick Ferguson, Mike Walsh and, of course, myself.

We were famously known as The Magnificent Seven. Unfortunately I was the first one to get shot. It proved to be unlucky thirteen for me when I got injured in my thirteenth appearance against Ipswich Town. I thought I would be out for a long time but I recovered quicker than anyone expected. Everton were due to play Middlesbrough on the Wednesday and I didn't make that. But Manchester City were next up on the Saturday so on Thursday I declared myself fit.

And that's where my problems began. Howard was having none of it and demanded that I travelled with the reserves to Newcastle the following day to get myself match fit. Not bloody likely, I thought. And I told him in no uncertain terms that he could forget packing me off with the 'stiffs'.

'I'm fit,' I said to Howard. 'I have no need to play in the reserves. I want to get back in the first team for the weekend.'

Howard just looked at me and then in the quickest U-turn of my life he agreed I didn't have to go. Then, amazingly, in the next breath he changed his mind again and went back to his original plan, ordering me to be on the team bus the following morning at 11 a.m. for the trip to Newcastle.

My mind was clear enough. I wasn't going and I

fucked off back to the Holiday Inn in Liverpool. I was fuming and went over and over what he had said. I wasn't taking this shit from him. So in a temper I went back to the club's Bellefield training ground that afternoon to sort it out once and for all. I had to wait a few hours. Howard was on a long lunch but when he returned I repeated my position that I wasn't going to Newcastle with the bloody reserves. He said something that was strange, accusing me of trying to work my passage out of the club.

'You've been tapped up anyway,' he said. 'I have had West Ham on the phone and other teams have rung about you.'

I didn't know what the hell he was talking about. I had no desire to leave Everton. But I never made that team bus on the Friday. I didn't bother going to training, either, or turn up for the City game on the Saturday. Sod that. I stayed in the hotel the whole weekend and walked into Bellefield bright and breezy on that Monday morning as if nothing had happened.

I changed and was immediately told by Howard's number two, Colin Harvey, that I wasn't allowed to train with the first team. My punishment was to work with the youth team. Fair enough. If he wanted to be that petty I'd play the game. But after training I went to see Howard again.

'I'm fining you two weeks' wages,' he told me. 'Do you believe what you did was wrong?'

'No,' I replied. 'I'm a man of my own principles.' Well aware, of course, that that stance usually ended up in me cutting my own throat.

My honesty obviously shocked him and he added, 'Right, you are in the first team against Liverpool on Saturday.'

The following morning I was back in the fold, training again with the first team. But not for much longer. I didn't stop working my bollocks off and even though we were given Wednesday off, I still went in for a sauna. Colin Harvey was in there as well. He was one of the greatest of all Everton players. Harvey, Alan Ball, Howard Kendall. That was a great midfield for Everton and, in honesty, there's never been a better one. Colin was a marvellous player and the perfect right-hand man for Howard. I looked up to him because he had done it all in the game of football. He was a tremendous servant to Everton football club. You don't get much better in terms of Goodison legends.

I think he had a soft spot for me, too. 'I admire you, Mickey,' he said. 'You might be wrong in what you do but you stick to your principles. You believe in what you do and I really admire that in you.'

I nodded, very much in agreement. He was right, of course, and I was back on a high. I met our captain Billy Wright for a game of pool and I was sinking a few balls when Howard grabbed mine in a manner of speaking. 'Hey, you. My office now,' he barked.

Christ, I'd gone from Mickey Thomas his big signing to 'Hey, you.'

Sat behind his desk, he told me, 'I'm going to call it a day.'

'You are doing a good job,' I chirped. 'You don't have to go.'

Astonished, he replied, 'No, not me. You. You are the one going. Your boots are packed.'

Obviously he hadn't seen the funny side. Not that I had anything to smile about now as he explained there was a private plane at Speke Airport ready to fly me down south to my new club, Brighton.

My short and not so sweet spell at Everton was over after just thirteen appearances. To this day I still joke when I am asked why I didn't stay longer at Goodison. I reply: 'Because every time I went down the tunnel I kept on hearing that bloody *Z-Cars* theme tune welcoming the players onto the pitch and it made me run the other way. I thought the cops were after me.'

I didn't know anything about Brighton. Thank God, I wasn't driving because I'd never have found the place. I thought it was New Brighton just down the coast from me in Colwyn Bay. Mind you, I wasn't joking when I said I wasn't going to sign for them. I'd just got a house in Liverpool and the carpets had just been fitted. I never moved in . . .

Back at my hotel, I told my wife Debbie to start packing. She never flinched. She was a lovely girl who had won a few beauty contests. A very stunning woman. Blonde. Very good looking. She would have been a top WAG, pictured in every newspaper, if I had been playing today.

Within an hour of my final meeting with Howard I was sitting in this little six-seater plane with my missus, bound for the south coast and another part of my life. Obviously, Howard was deadly serious in selling me.

Debbie supported me in this new chapter in our lives, although I was still adamant that I wouldn't rush into signing for Brighton. OK, I'd go along for the ride but I resisted signing on the dotted line – until they plied me with enough drink to get me to change my mind.

Touch down. We arrived in Brighton. And that was the start of months of mayhem. All down to me, need I add. I felt my career was spiralling out of control. From Manchester United to Everton. Now on to Brighton. I was totally frustrated. From out of nowhere I now had a reputation for hopping from one club to another. I didn't like that one bit. It gave the impression, wrongly, that I was a bad lad. A trouble-maker. I wasn't. But I couldn't escape from the fact that I was fast becoming a footballing gypsy. That was only because of my fall-out with Howard Kendall and the fact that I didn't want to join Brighton.

What a disaster – mainly for Brighton. I admit I well and truly fucked them. I knew Brighton wasn't the place for me. My career was out of control and not even the broad smile of Jimmy Melia, who met me at the airport, could make me feel at home. Jimmy was a legend in football, having played for ten years for Liverpool in the fifties and sixties and who now worked as a Brighton scout and was loved by Bill Shankly. Jimmy played for England and he later became a marvellous manager, taking Brighton to the 1983 FA Cup Final. I must admit I sat in awe of him on the journey to the Brighton hotel where I would be staying.

Walking through the reception, my eyes fixed onto a TV set, which was showing the latest sports news, one headline obviously caught my attention: MICKY THOMAS SIGNS FOR BRIGHTON. Oh no I hadn't. I hadn't put pen to any piece of paper even though they were throwing loads of cash at players. They offered me big money and I could have doubled my Everton wages by just saying 'Yes'. They had big stars, too. Jimmy Case, for example, who had such a fabulous Liverpool career and shot to fame with that all-conquering Kop side of the 1970s. Jimmy became known as the player with one of the hardest shots in the game and enjoyed two spells at Brighton.

There was also Michael Robinson, Neil McNab, and Steve Foster, their big captain, who also had two stints at Brighton, playing almost three hundred games. He had a huge heart and was an inspirational leader. And, like Jimmy, he became a great drinking buddy.

After a restless night in that Brighton hotel, Foster and Case met me at the training ground and asked me if I was going to sign. I just shook my head. The club wanted me badly and had no hesitation in agreeing a £500,000 fee with Everton. I still didn't fancy the uprooting, even more so when their good old secretary Ken Calver told me to go inside the stadium and look around. Look around? There was one stand. Now that was really going to make me sign for the club.

I definitely played hard to get and that night the club made one final push. Jimmy Melia took me out to see Dr Hook. He even brought his dancing shoes and wore a white suit. I couldn't stop laughing. He shoved more than a few drinks down my neck and in a moment of weakness I agreed to sign.

The next morning I went into my first training session and met my new team-mates. That night I was out on the tiles again with Foster and Case. We went to some charity bash at a nightclub and I swear I nearly died of alcohol poisoning. It was free wine all night. White wine. And I must have drunk the equivalent of a French vineyard all by myself.

I just drank and drank and drank. All I remember is getting out of someone's car back at my hotel. I was absolutely legless. Needless to say, I never made training the next day. I was still in my stinking pit at 1 p.m. And what a mess I was in. I had been sick everywhere when I came to my senses. Sick in every room of my hotel pad and stupidly I did almost die: I came close to choking on my own vomit.

I can still see myself now lying in a pool of sick. It kept oozing out of my mouth and I couldn't get to my feet. I just remember thinking: Don't go to sleep, Mickey. Don't pass out and choke on this mess.

I fought against closing my eyes until I managed to crawl to the bathroom and get myself cleaned up. Stupid sod.

Two hours later I got a taxi to the training ground and I was told to report to the manager, Mike Bailey. I was in trouble again. He'd just signed me forty-eight hours earlier and there was this smelly wreck in his office, a star signing who had yet to kick a ball in anger. No surprise then that he immediately asked me where I had been.

'To be honest, gaffer,' I slurred, 'I got pissed.'

'I know,' he said. 'You've been out with Foster and Case and I'm afraid I've got to fine you for breaking club rules.'

Christ. It was only my second day as a Brighton player and I was in the shit. Hit big style in my back pocket. He didn't have any option, to be fair, but his discipline didn't do anything to control my behaviour.

Far from it. I went on to play just twenty games for Brighton and scored one goal when the ball hit me on the head by accident and went in. They sold me ten months later for £200,000.

In that time, I went missing on a regular basis, rarely turning up for training or for matches. I flew off to Spain more than once because I couldn't handle it again. I had to get away. I was in Wrexham one day to watch the boys and I saw *Football Focus* on the TV in the bar at the Racecourse Ground.

I was mentioned, of course. Mickey Thomas had gone missing and Brighton couldn't find him. My mate Joey Jones, standing beside me, piped up, 'He's not missing – he's here with me.'

I felt at home back at Wrexham. And it was good to be with Joey who, like me, was watching the lads. He didn't agree with me pissing off from Brighton but he knew why.

Just in case they released the tracker dogs, I flew back to Spain the next morning and when I eventually went home to Colwyn Bay, Mike Bailey drove up to speak to me. He begged me to return and I did. But I was in no mood to buckle down and commit myself to the club. I disappeared so much I was like the Lord Lucan of football. I too could vanish easily without trace, much to Mike's ultimate frustration.

Poor bloke. He bent over backwards but eventually he admitted in the club programme on Saturday 24 April 1982, before the Manchester United game: 'We feel that we have gone out of our way to help the player and allow him to settle his domestic affairs. But now I feel we have been completely let down and for me . . . enough is enough.'

It wasn't so much a case of sorting out my home life. He'd got that wrong. I felt the only way I could get my release from Brighton was by going missing on a regular basis. Eventually, I thought, they would get so pissed off they'd get rid of me. I was trying to force their hand, to get them to get their finger out and let me go. I just didn't want to be at Brighton.

They paid all that good money but I should never have been daft enough to sign in the first place. I did feel sorry for Mike because I put the manager under a huge amount of pressure. I didn't care at that time. I was obsessed in getting away from the club. That's why Spain became a regular bolthole. I would book myself in for a week or so in a hotel in Marbella just to get away from all the pressures back in England. I did a lot of walking on the beach, a lot of thinking. And a lot of drinking in the bars around the millionaires' paradise of Peurto Banus. Rubbing shoulders with the rich and wealthy – without having two halfpennies to rub together myself.

The more I thought about my life in Brighton the more I hit the bottle. Drinking to excess was easy when no one really knew who I was. I must admit it brought a smile to my face when I read the English papers, which were full of missing Mickey stories. I'm here, I used to say to myself. And I was glad to be on the Costa del Sol instead of losing my mind in Brighton. I didn't suffer one bit of guilt. Eventually after I got bored with the high life I would fly back to the south coast.

But I never settled. A couple of weeks later I would repeat the disappearing act, piss off for another fortnight in the sun. On one return, probably my last, I got back after training when the boys had finished. I quickly took off my clothes and jumped into the bath with them. No one else was laughing when I was summoned to see the manager.

My response: 'What's his name, by the way?'

I didn't give a sod. I know I made Mike's life hell but I still don't blame myself even to this day. I blame Brighton. They put pressure on me to sign when in my heart I knew I didn't want to commit. Anyway, it was clear it was the end of the Brighton line for me. My last game was against Ipswich and I told the gaffer I didn't want to play. But they had to play me to sell me, so that my next club could see I was fit and still a worthwhile investment. So I took to the field with cotton wool in my ears.

I knew I would get stick and sure enough the abuse came my way thick and fast. Not that I heard much of it. Ten minutes later the cotton wool came out. The fans were back singing my name again because they knew I had given everything, even though I was about to leave the club high and dry. My time was up. There had been far too many headlines of MISFIT THOMAS GOES MISSING, HALF A MILLION QUID AND HE DOESN'T TURN UP FOR TRAINING.

Well, the headline writers could put their pens away now. I was off. But not before one final unexpected act on my part. When the contract was finally sorted and I was released, I refused to take the signing-on fee, which was due to me. I told them to keep the money. I was entitled to £25,000 but I didn't take a penny from them.

It was a rash gesture on my part for all the trouble I had caused Brighton. I wasn't going to take the piss entirely and pocket a hefty cheque I didn't believe I warranted. That was one hell of an expensive way to say sorry.

Eight

So with my time up at Brighton – and who can blame them; my behaviour had been quite extraordinary – I was off.

Stoke City came in for me very late, just before the start of the new season. I had been training by myself for the whole of the summer: running for hours on the beach at Colwyn Bay, keeping myself fit for the next new challenge. I knew there would be one. And, sure enough, I got a call from Brighton to tell me that Stoke wanted to talk to me.

Although Richie Barker was the manager of Stoke I met his assistant, Bill Asprey, at Knutsford services in Cheshire, because my new boss was tied up on another matter. As he was offering me the deal, Asprey told me that Richie had always been a big fan of mine and that he was desperate to sign me.

I already knew that my old Manchester United pal Sammy McIlroy was on board and he was still a great player. They also had a young Paul Bracewell, who would later star for Newcastle and Sunderland and play for England. He was also a member of the Everton Championship-winning side in the mid-eighties. So the midfield looked pretty strong.

Bill told me that as far as Richie was concerned, I was one player to complete his future planning. He said Richie was impressed with my playing record and was a big admirer of my ability. 'You have got a great left foot,' said Bill. 'He knows all about your skill on the ball and your talent of producing the right cross at the right time.'

They had obviously done their homework. Bill said I was the kind of tenacious player they loved. A true left-winger. And I had goals in me, too. I could give them the balance they craved. I could dribble, I could pass, I could score. I was their man, then.

I shook on the deal, only to get a telephone call at home from the Chelsea chairman Ken Bates. I will always remember the conversation.

'Are you Mickey Thomas?'

'Yes, I am.'

'Well, I've been told not to touch you by a lot of people in the game. You have a bad reputation, always drinking and out shagging. But my manager still wants to sign you.'

I told him that his information was spot on. He told me to meet him the next night at 8 p.m. in the Piccadilly Hotel, Manchester, to discuss a move to Chelsea.

I agreed, put down the phone and immediately thought, I'm not signing for you, you twat! I had already shaken hands on the deal to take me to Stoke and, anyway, I didn't like the way he had spoken to me. I didn't like his attitude. Not a lot do.

By all accounts Ken wasn't very happy when I kept my word in signing for Stoke and not turning up for the planned meeting. Did this face look bothered? Not one bit.

So it was on to Stoke which at least geographically was a lot nearer to my Colwyn Bay home.

The first game of the season was against Arsenal at home. I wore the number-ten shirt and was delighted to play alongside players like Sammy Mac, Paul Bracewell and Mark Chamberlain, who was making his debut and would become a relevation for a short period. There was also Dave Watson, the old England centre-half, so it was a good side.

We ended up winning 2–1. I had a great game and was named Man of the Match. I had been desperate to succeed and become an instant hit with Stoke. I felt it was a great start to my career – a performance capped by making a goal for George Berry. We were all buzzing after the game. Although I didn't score I was still more than chuffed with my performance.

I was happy that the Stoke fans took to me straight away, too. I wasn't daft. Sometimes it can be difficult there if you are an ex-Manchester United player, but I knew how to get them on my side early on.

That's when Lee Chapman came onto the Mickey radar. He was a former Stoke striker who had moved to Arsenal and he was a figure of hate for leaving the Potteries. When a former player comes back to his old club they are always immediately cast as the villain. And it was no different for Lee Chapman.

I thought that the best way to introduce myself to Stoke fans would be to nobble Chapman at the earliest opportunity. And I did. It took just twenty minutes.

Chapman was turning just in front of the dug-out with the ball when I launched myself at him, giving him a right whack. Ouch. He slumped to the ground, writhing in agony, and all you could hear were the Stoke fans singing, 'There's only one Mickey Thomas.'

So they were right behind me straight away, which was great to hear. I had a fantastic season, one of my most enjoyable. I finished it as top goalscorer and missed only one game through injury. As a team Stoke played the best football the supporters had seen for a long while and also finished in their highest Division One position for some years.

We battered teams and scored goals for fun. Even the great Stanley Matthews, Stoke's most famous son, couldn't get enough of it. To think that a great skilful winger like Stanley appreciated our style of play was something to be proud of. He would come up to me and

HAPPY DAYS That's me right at the front with some neat shorts and sandals with my mum and dad above my left shoulder.

FAB FOUR I'd give everything for those curls now as brothers Phillip (on my right) and Kevin and sister Pauline smile for this great family shot.

BOYS OWN One of my first football teams showing off our new kit on a pitch near my Mochdre home.

OH MAN I looked good in the colours of Manchester United during my first season.

WREX 'EM Blimey I was proud to be a member of this fabulous Wrexham squad, possibly the best ever in the club's history.

BEST MAN Here I am with more hair than George Best at a testimonial for the great Gareth Davies.

GO MAN GO Another defender bites the dust as I display my dribbling skills in the FA Cup Final against Arsenal at Wembley.

GLORY DAYS Superstars, superstars wherever you look, so I don't know why I'm looking so glum in this Manchester United official line-up.

STAM THE MAN It's back to that familiar pose, this time in a Chelsea shirt at Stamford Bridge when I first signed.

OVER HERE
Seems I've got plenty to shout about in my Chelsea playing days against rivals Tottenham.

DOUBLE TROUBLE
Easy does it as I'm pictured scoring my second goal on my Chelsea debut against Sheffield Wednesday.

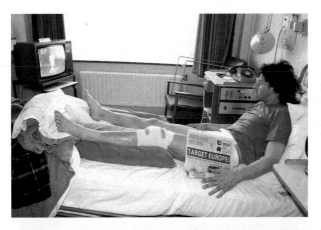

CROCK OF GOLD
Time to put my feet up after a knee operation. Not like me to be that still.

CHEERS That's me celebrating after clinching promotion for Chelsea.

SPACK AND SPIN
Nigel Spackman leaves it to me as I head for goal in my Chelsea hey day.

CITY SLICKERS Another media day and another new line-up, this time with this great Stoke City team.

MICKEY
THOMAS
Stoke City

ON THE BALL
I don't look very mobile
but I definitely was in
my spell at Stoke.

PROUD AS PUNCH
One of my early games
for Wales when I was
clearly in the mood to
represent my country.

YANKEE DOODLE
DANDY Enjoying the
good life in the States
with plenty of champagne
and hair flowing.

GUNNED DOWN
The calm before the storm
on that famous day when
little Wrexham humbled
mighty Arsenal and Tony
Adams in the FA Cup.

OLD PALS' ACT
Me and my big pal
Joey Jones as Joey shows
he's a much better player
when the boots aren't
on his feet.

tell me how much he enjoyed watching my football. He even said that he wished he was still able to play because he would love to be out there for just ten minutes – praise doesn't come much higher than that.

When I was injured for one game I was sitting watching from one of the hospitality boxes when there was a knock at the door. It was Stanley Matthews asking if I was around. I couldn't believe it: here was one of the greatest players football has ever known looking to have a chat with me, Mickey Thomas, a cheeky chappy from the back streets of North Wales.

That's about as good as it got because thanks to Richie Barker experiencing a walk along the road to Damascus – the wrong way – during the summer, things were about to take a huge turn for the worse.

Richie went on a course involving the FA's contro-versial coach Charles Hughes, who was a disciple of the long-ball game: kick it as far as you can and pick up the pieces. Well, far from seeing the light, Stoke City was plunged into gloom, as Richie seemed brainwashed by this so-called FA guru.

Myself, Sammy Mac and Paul Bracewell were called over by Richie during pre-season training one day. He told us that he would be changing our style of play for the new season. He explained that just like Watford under Graham Taylor had been doing we were going to strike the ball long, always aiming for the opposition eighteen-yard box. We would have to sprint on to feed off the rebounds. He justified this madness by telling us that Hughes's manual proves that you get more goals by this method. We just looked at him, stunned. We knew that as midfielders we were simply going to be by-passed as the ball was thumped over our heads towards goal.

It just sent me loopy. I couldn't handle it. We were playing warm-up games in Sweden and I kept walking off the pitch during the matches. I just shouted out, 'I'm not bloody playing, I'm not getting a ruddy kick!'

I would get onto the team bus, not caring about the consequences. I just couldn't put up with what was happening.

The situation didn't get any better off the pitch, either. Because of what I had achieved in my first season at Stoke, I was due a £100-a-week bonus once the new season started. But after what had gone on in pre-season Richie told me that I wouldn't be getting the money after all.

We were due to play at Everton on the opening day and were staying at a hotel when Richie broke the news about the non-payment of the bonus to me. I told him to stuff it, I wouldn't be playing at Goodison Park then. I was angry and gave him a volley of expletives. They had reneged on a deal and that was completely out of order. He told me if I played against Everton then the club would try to sort something out after the game.

Wales manager Mike England was watching the game. We lost 3–1 and with the new tactics the ball was zooming over my head. I almost went off with neck ache! Mike told me I would have to get away from Stoke if this was to continue because I would never see the ball, considering most of the time it was in the sky. It was a huge contrast to the previous season. I wasn't enjoying a minute of this new campaign. That was reflected in my attitude on the pitch. I was collecting loads of bookings and being sent off. I just took out my frustration about our new tactics on my opponents' legs. I couldn't get my head around what Richie was playing at.

We just didn't play to our strengths. I lost my head on countless occasions because I couldn't make an impact on the game. There was no decline in my skill level. I just couldn't get into the game any more because of the barrage of long, high balls. I, Sammy Mac, and the rest of our footballing players were pissed off. We had one team meeting when everyone said the system wasn't working. It was shit football. The paint on the walls blistered as every one of us let our feelings be known. But Richie was having none of it. That was the new Stoke way, we were told. We had to stick to the new system.

How misguided could you get? Richie was a lovely guy but he just got it completely wrong. It was like playing one-twos with God.

The fans quickly cottoned on to what was happening. There was unrest within the camp and on the terraces but Richie wouldn't turn the clock back and he was to pay for his stubbornness by being sacked. Bill Asprey took over the reins temporarily but by then it was virtually all over for me. He wanted to stamp his authority on the team and that meant getting rid of me because he looked upon me as a troublemaker. It might not have helped my cause that instead of joining the rest of my team-mates in the players' lounge after games I would be out in some of the hardest pubs in the Stoke area with members of the notorious gang of Stoke City fans, 'The Naughty Forties'.

I knew they had a bad reputation and would get involved in battles with supporters from other clubs but I enjoyed their company. They were great to me, and in any case, nothing nasty happened when I was with them, although it must have seemed a strange sight: a Division One footballer with a gang of hard cases, some might even say nutters. We would just have a few drinks together. I must admit, though, I was glad they were on my side – I wouldn't have fancied having a row with any of them. They could see at the end how frustrated I had become with my lot playing for Stoke and they understood. They didn't like the style of football either.

They would have pictures of me on their walls at home. They were just chuffed that I would mix with them. It did me good, too, because I could relate to their lives. They would play a major part on my life, too. In fact, I'm still in touch with some members of The Naughty Forties even now. A great bloke, Mark Chester, who is better known as Jasper, is someone I can always rely on. Let's just say he is someone who is very useful to know when you are having one or two problems with people. He had a big reputation in those days with football hooliganism, which was at its height then. But Jasper is a reformed character now. He's still Stoke City mad and will be enjoying his club's return to the top flight of English football after a twenty-three-year absence.

Jasper is actually concentrating on the football now instead of looking for like-minded opposition fans for street battles. There was another lad called Salty who I also got to know well. Plus Cockney Ted and his son Danny and also Ian 'Skin' Dyer and Cossack. They all paid me the biggest compliment possible when they turned up at my testimonial game against Wolves in 1997, even though it clashed with Stoke's last ever game at the Victoria Ground.

I don't think Ted and Danny had ever missed a Stoke game in their lives but they came over to support me and I will forever be in their debt for that. The nearest I came to returning the compliment was later joining them all on a trip to Birmingham City. It was one of the best experiences I have ever had and left me with an idea that should be put into action now. I stood with the lads at the back of the stand behind one of the goals at St Andrews when the thought came to me: what an education this would be for some of the pampered players who are blissfully unaware of the emotions of the people who follow them all over the country. If I had ever become a manager in the professional game I would have stuck anyone not giving everything among the crowd at a game. There could be no better reality check. Imagine it. These footballers rubbing shoulders with supporters who live and breathe every game. It would make them see first hand what it means to the ordinary fan. How much a defeat hurts them. It would be the perfect kick up the pampered backside of any player who was simply going through the motions. Maybe some of today's managers should consider using this shock tactic, patented by Mickey T.

The Naughty Forties brought a smile to my face when I reacted so badly to Stoke's switch of style. But I don't bear any grudge against Richie. As a bloke he was OK. It was just that he allowed himself to be brainwashed by that idiot Charles Hughes.

I remember Richie calling it as it was. He used to say I was a scallywag, that I would be out all night but would then be first in the queue for training. I can't argue with that. It's just that it could have turned out so differently with Stoke.

Nine

I might have been miles and miles from Colwyn Bay, but as far as playing football was concerned Chelsea well and truly became my spiritual home. I loved my time there, although, true to form, the action wasn't always confined to the pitch.

The biggest surprise was actually having the opportunity to sign for them in the first place after upsetting Ken Bates, the all-powerful and outspoken chairman, who normally doesn't give anyone a sniff of a second chance.

Chelsea, you remember, had come in for me when I was leaving Brighton but by then I had already shaken hands on the deal that would see me joining Stoke City. Twenty eventful months later their manager – and my old boss – John Neal got back in touch with me. I fancied going this time around.

After all, John knew all about me, and my big mate Joey Jones was already at Stamford Bridge. Another Wrexham old boy, Eddie Niedzwiecki was also there.

I met John at the Watford Gap services on the M1. He quickly reminded me that I had taken the piss out of Bates the last time and now he wanted me at his house to sort out the transfer. Mind, I could have messed things up again even before I had put pen to paper.

That night I stayed with John and the next morning he drove me over to the chairman's home and we all got into Ken's luxury Rolls-Royce for the trip to Stamford Bridge. Near the ground there was this lovely girl on a zebra crossing waving at the car. I blurted out that I wouldn't mind giving her one. Bates quickly explained that she was his son's future wife. Bloody hell, I thought, I've done it again!

Anyway, he was OK about everything that had gone on previously. In fact, the only stipulation Bates made was that I had to move house nearer to London. So I did, moving all the way from Colwyn Bay to Rhyl, a few miles down the North Wales Coast!

Playing-wise things got off to a great start. My first game was away to Derby and we won 1–0. Sheffield Wednesday were next up at Stamford Bridge.

I was in the hotel bar the night before the game – I never needed much sleep being hyperactive – with the physio Jimmy Hendry. I just had a few beers. When I woke up the next day I felt really ill. I was suffering from a migraine, something I had never experienced before. I arrived at the ground and went straight to the physio's room and told Norman Medhurst I couldn't play, I felt terrible. But this was a vital Second Division promotion game. Wednesday were top and we were second. There would be 38,000 at the Bridge.

Anyway, they massaged me, did everything they could, and somehow I was able to get on the pitch. I ended up scoring twice and making the other goal in a 3–2 win. There I was in the Sunday newspapers, anointed: MICKEY THOMAS, KING OF THE KING'S ROAD.

On Monday I had once again grabbed the headlines but this time for negative reasons.

The Sheffield Wednesday manager, Howard Wilkinson really seemed to have it in for me – although he later ended up signing me. He told the newspaper guys that I was a great player but only until I got fed up with the manager. Then, Wilkinson added, 'he will bugger off!'

He absolutely slaughtered me. In fact, with him around whenever we faced Sheffield Wednesday it seemed to all go off.

I enjoyed a great rapport with the fans. It was an exciting time because we ended up winning the Second Division Championship which meant that Chelsea would be back amongst the big boys. The Chelsea fans had been through some barren times. But at last they had something to shout about.

For Joey and me it was fantastic, two local lads from North Wales being idolised by The Shed. Better still,

John Neal allowed us to travel and not put down any roots in London.

We would stay occasionally – and I will tell you about some of those memorable overnights a little later. Mostly, though, it was motorways are us. A typical day would see me leave Colwyn Bay at 5.30 a.m. and get to Joey's Wrexham home at about 6 a.m. We would share the driving and be in training for 10.30 a.m. After training we would jump into the car and head off home again.

One day we were heading through Whitchurch and absolutely fed up of another day's travelling ahead of us when we heard there had been a big crash on the M1. Quick as a flash we got on the phone to John Neal and told him the M1 was blocked. Yes, said John, he had heard that on the radio but it was the north-bound lanes – the opposite direction to which we were heading – and to get our arses down there as quickly as possible!

As I have said, there were occasions when we stayed down south. Sometimes we would plonk ourselves down in the physio's room or even the referee's room at Stamford Bridge.

If I was there I wasn't often alone, preferring some female company to pass the night-time hours!

One night, when I was staying with this girl, I decided to switch on the Stamford Bridge floodlights. It was the night before we were due to play a live game against Everton.

I couldn't resist it: I had to christen the centre-circle spot with the help of my female companion. So the next day, when we were about to kick-off, I was busy telling everyone what I had done to some girl in this area of the pitch the night before.

Sometimes, even if I was by myself, I would still switch the floodlights on and have a kickabout. Some of my best goals were scored at the Bridge with no one else around!

To be fair to John Neal, he never once tried to make me move down permanently because he knew that no matter what I had been up to I could run all day on a football pitch. Even if I had been out all night, I would never ever let anyone down out on the pitch.

I confess, there were occasions when I nearly didn't make it through my own fault. Sometimes that would be because I had taken full advantage of the facilities offered by the famous Stringfellows nightclub. At one stage they even had a picture of me in there. I was a real Jack the lad in those days, even though deep down I still preferred my home life.

But after one session at Stringfellows I turned up at training the next day feeling really ill. I told the physio that I couldn't train. He said there was nothing wrong with me, and to prove it he stuck a thermometer into my mouth. Luckily, he had to go out of the room and so to try to prove that I was suffering I boiled a kettle, dipped the thermometer into it and then into my mouth. The physio returned just as the thermometer was in the process of blowing up. He was startled and yelled, 'Christ, I'd better call an ambulance!' But he quickly realised what I had done and, luckily for me, saw the funny side of it.

Of course, we weren't on the massive wages that today's footballers earn, so I doubt whether Joey and I could have afforded to live in London even if we'd wanted to. But going home was our bit of karma. No one, though, questioned our abilities. If I ever thought my game was being affected then I wouldn't have done what I did.

Maybe some of my Chelsea team-mates at the time might have resented us being allowed to go home all the time. You certainly wouldn't get away with that in today's more disciplined climate.

When we did stay in London we went from the ridiculous to the sublime. If it wasn't the various rooms within Stamford Bridge it would sometimes be a £10-a-night hostel for the homeless or, at the other extreme, the swanky environs of an Arab-owned palace in the most fashionable part of London.

A mate of ours had the keys to the Arab palace. We were once based there for a night out at Stringfellows. George Michael and Andrew Ridgeley of Wham! were going on to a party and someone asked me why wasn't I going? He told me to go down the alley where I would find George Michael. Sure enough there he was, sitting in a big limo with a girl. He wound down the window and told me and Joey to get in and join him.

It was a great night and I ended up with some Wham! records. There were pop people all over the place: Paul Young, who was huge at the time, was there too.

The next day John Neal was about to go off on one because he knew I had been out drinking. I told him where I had been and he shut up once I had handed over some of the Wham! stuff.

I used to get away with murder when good old John was the gaffer. Once we were playing a game in the north-west and we were staying in a Cheshire hotel. Luckily, I was on the first floor so I was able to sneak out of the bedroom window to go and meet some girl.

The next morning I was coming into the hotel at 7 a.m. when I bumped into John Neal. I thought I was going to cop it but luckily he knew I was generally an early-riser and thought I had just come in from a stroll.

'Lovely morning, Mickey,' he said.

'Fantastic, Gaffer,' I replied with huge relief. Phew. That was definitely a close one. I was almost caught with my pants down, literally.

So you can imagine my surprise when I discovered that my gaffer was at the centre of his own sex scandal.

It came one morning when we picked up a copy of the *Sun* on our way to training and there was my 'dad' John plastered all over the front page – never mind the back page. Evidently, he had been playing away with some girl who had dished the dirt on him to millions of readers.

As you can imagine, Joey and I lapped up every word, hardly believing what we were reading. Then we almost collapsed in tears when the girl revealed that they would often make love to classical music. That was it. We couldn't wait for the gaffer's appearance in the dressing room that morning. Just as he came in Joey and myself started humming a well-known classical tune. Probably, quite appropriately, something from 'The Nutcracker Suite'. I don't know if John saw the funny side of it but we certainly did. The dressing room can be a cruel place at times.

Yes, I had a real ball off the pitch at Stamford Bridge. And I really enjoyed myself playing for Chelsea on it, too. Joey and I were treated brilliantly by the fans because I think they could see that really we were just like they were. There was great camaraderie around the place and I love going back to Chelsea to this day.

Mind, once the fans almost got me in hot water. We were drawn against Sheffield Wednesday in the League Cup. The first game at Stamford Bridge ended all square, but as we were going down the tunnel one of their lads, Andy Blair, said something sarcastic to me. I didn't really hear it and so I let it go.

In the replay at Hillsborough we were 3–0 down and this guy Blair starts abusing one of our players, Nigel Spackman. I told him to leave it out and in any case why bother as Wednesday were 3–0 up.

Later, we got a corner in front of our travelling army of 7,000 Chelsea fans. As everyone was concentrating on the corner kick I laid Andy Blair spark out in the penalty area.

Some of the Sheffield Wednesday players suspected I'd done it but no one saw the punch. The referee came up to me and asked me if I hit him, which I of course denied. Suddenly the Chelsea fans erupted into 'There's only one Mickey Thomas'. Obviously, some of them had seen what had happened. I motioned to them to be quiet. Anyway, I got off it and at half-time John Neal asked me why I had hit him. I told the gaffer Blair had insulted my wife. He said fair enough then and told us we were all in a mess and to get out of it.

We ended up drawing 4–4 and won the second replay 2–1, which meant a two-legged semi-final against Sunderland. We ended up going out of the competition and our fans rioted at Stamford Bridge. There was never a dull moment.

John Neal started to have problems and he needed major surgery, which forced him further and further into the background at the club. John Hollins, a former player, took over and he didn't have the same ideas as John Neal when it came to me.

For a start, John Hollins didn't like me travelling and wanted me to move south. When I didn't I found myself not playing any more on a regular basis. One day at training Hollins told me I had better go and see the chairman at the ground. 'Don't you mean the fucking manager?' I said, because in my opinion, Hollins had become Ken Bates's puppet when it came to team decisions.

When I got to the ground Bates told me that he had a few offers on the table for me and it was a chance for me to make a few bob. There were three clubs in for me: Leeds United, Birmingham and West Brom.

He said that funnily enough the West Brom manager, Johnny Giles, was staying in a hotel just down the road and that I could go and meet him if I wanted to. I asked Bates what the alternatives were. He said there weren't any because I wasn't prepared to move to London. I told him he was wrong to question my commitment to Chelsea and that I loved the club.

John Hollins, though, wanted his own team and had started to dismantle the old one. He eventually paid the ultimate price for ripping the side up: the sack.

So when I met Johnny Giles the writing was already on the wall as far as Chelsea was concerned.

One thing that made my hair stand up on end was a comment that famous World Cup winner Nobby Stiles made to me when he was at West Brom. I had just played for the Baggies against Chelsea at The Hawthorns and the travelling Chelsea fans had given me a great reception.

Nobby told me: 'I've won the World Cup, I've won

the European Cup but I've never seen a player get that sort of adulation from visiting fans like you have.'

That summed it all up really: what Chelsea meant to me and what I meant to the fans.

Ten

Obviously, I've had my problems with managers. Loved some but didn't see eye to eye with others. But there wasn't a moment's hesitation when I agreed to sign for Johnny Giles at West Brom in 1985. He was a bit of a hero of mine. A great player, too, and the kind of man you meet in life and never forget. It was a pity, then, that our time together at The Hawthorns was cut so dramatically short.

But I'm jumping ahead of myself, as usual. Before I spoke to Johnny, I bumped into West Brom's chairman Sid Lucas in the reception of some London hotel. They all look the same to me. His greeting was warm and welcoming. 'Oh Mickey,' he said, shaking me fiercely by the hand. 'You have got to sign for West Brom. You are my son's favourite player. Please sign for us.'

The chairman loved me. And so did my new manager, who was about to offer me a dream role at the Baggies: football without training. Bliss. I found him upstairs in his room and Giles said: 'Will you sign for me? I'm a big fan of yours, Mickey. You don't even have to turn up for training. Just show for the matches. I just want you to play for us. You are the type of player we need at this club. We're in real trouble and we need to get out of it. You're the player to help us do that.'

In truth, I didn't really want to sign for West Brom. They were bottom of the table, in the shit. But I signed for Giles really because of my great respect for him as a player. I could see what direction he wanted to go with the club. Unfortunately, I didn't see that direction being towards the exit door in less time than it took to unpack my suitcase.

Anyway, there I was, officially a West Brom player with permission not to have to turn up at the training ground and who was allowed to live in Colwyn Bay, travelling to The Hawthorns for matches.

I met the West Brom players the following day, a Friday, and played my first game twenty-four hours later against Coventry City at Highfield Road. It wasn't the best of debuts for yours truly. I gave a penalty away after twenty minutes and we ended up losing the game 3–0. I trooped back to the dressing room, expecting the boss to go bananas, but I wasn't prepared for the resulting mayhem.

The whole team began arguing: with each other and with the gaffer. Garth Crooks doesn't say boo to a goose

in his TV interviews, but he let fly, along with Baggies'
team-mates Tony Grealish, Ally Robertson and Steve
Hunt. It went off all over the place. Everyone was effing
and blinding and Giles and my new team-mates didn't
hold back with the abuse.

I minded my own business, thinking it was just
another dressing-room bust-up. No one had a go at me
and I just kept quiet. I kept my head down. It was so
bizarre. The row went on for ages, and believe me it was
one hell of a barney. I just let them get on with it. But
Christ, it was vocal. I thought to myself, Fucking hell,
this is a good start to my Baggies career.

Unknown to me at the time, Giles resigned the
following morning. I'd only signed because of him and
he was off, barely three days into my West Brom career.
He did a runner faster than I ever did.

I never did take Giles up on his invitation to train on
my own. The chairman wouldn't have been too happy
with me if I had done DIY training back in Colwyn Bay.
I used to travel to the Midlands with Jimmy Nicholl who
lived in Warrington at the time. I didn't miss a day,
you'll be surprised to discover. But to be fair, I loved my
time at West Brom.

I got on great with all the players. They were a good
bunch. We had a fighting spirit. We were in it together.
And we had a load of laughs, too. I remember being in
the bath the day before the club signed George Riley. I
was with Steve Hunt, who later went on to play in

America. In fact, he was a huge star out there. A great player. Very good on the ball. Tenacious.

Carlton Palmer, an up-and-coming motor-mouth at the time, was in the bath with us. Myself and Steve joked that George was rubbish and Carlton piped up: 'Yeah, he is rubbish. What are we doing signing him?'

So the next day, George arrived – all six-foot-odd of him. Like the Incredible Hulk on stilts. I was the first to make friends and I joked that Carlton had given him a bit of stick. Carlton changed next to me in the dressing room and Big George came in and I said: 'Hey, Carlton, tell George what you were saying about him yesterday.'

Carlton almost turned white. He panicked and made a quick exit. He certainly moved faster than he did on the pitch. It was good fun winding up Carlton, and I must admit I couldn't have been happier playing in the famous stripes. The team didn't play that well but on a personal level my stint there couldn't have gone any better. In fact, I would have stayed longer it if it hadn't been for my main executioner – Ron Saunders.

But into the Baggies' breach before him stepped good old Nobby Stiles, who had sent me a telegram when I reached the FA Cup Final with his old club Manchester United. He told me I reminded him of himself. That was a great compliment coming from a European Cup and World Cup winner. I gave Nobby everything in his short reign at West Brom.

I played thirty matches out of thirty for West Brom.

But then Saunders took over, becoming my third Baggies' manager and I was about to see a major turn-around in events. I will never forget his first words when he came into the dressing room to meet the players.

'Right,' he barked, 'I'm the new manager. You can all call me a c*** if you want but you will have to pick your bollocks up afterwards.'

Fair enough, I thought. He's a hard man; I can live with that. How foolish of me. It quickly got to the stage where I couldn't stand the guy. That feeling of mutual loathing started the following morning when I turned up to training. I couldn't quite believe my ears, though, when the kit man told me there was a bit of a problem. I wasn't allowed in the first-team dressing room. Nor were Garth Crooks, Imre Varadi, Ally Robertson and few of the other boys.

'You are in the reserve dressing room,' said the kit man. 'The gaffer wants you to change in there.'

I couldn't believe it. I felt embarrassed more than anything – embarrassed for myself and for the boys.

We all got our kit on and the lads headed out for Saunders' first training session before me. Crooks and the boys were quickly stopped in their tracks.

'No, no,' said Saunders. 'You lot are not with us. You are over there in the reserves with Thomas.'

Well, I was never slow at coming forward. Never have been. So I pulled Saunders and said, 'What the fucking hell is going on here?'

He obviously had a problem with me living in Colwyn Bay and replied: 'If you don't move to the Midlands then you don't play.'

Up yours, mate. 'Well, that's sorted then, Gaffer,' I said. 'I won't play.'

Saunders was unmoved. Then again, nothing would crack that hard face of his. What he said next, though, stunned me: 'Don't tell anyone that you won't be playing at Old Trafford on Saturday.'

I agreed. I wouldn't say anything. I wouldn't say a word that I was axed from the Manchester United game.

I just walked out of the training ground, straight into a posse of pressmen, and gave them their exclusive for the day.

'The manager won't let me train with the first team, boys,' I casually informed them.

Headlines again, then. The fans went mad. They sprayed a slogan at the back of the stand declaring, 'Thomas In, Saunders Out.' War had broken out and there would only be one winner.

I just couldn't work out why he wouldn't play me. Why would he not play his best players. It obviously became a massive problem, but more for Saunders than me. I didn't figure in his plans. Fair enough, I suppose.

We didn't see eye to eye. He couldn't handle me because I wasn't that bothered about him. I just wanted to play football and he wouldn't let me. One by one,

Saunders phased out all the senior players, but for some reason I was still around when the season came to an end and we were at the beginning of a new campaign.

I had had enough and I told him to his miserable face: 'Get me sold.'

I wasn't prepared to play reserve football. But I was still prepared to keep myself fit – and winding up Saunders in the process.

The first day back at training we were packed off to this park for running up a mountain where Saunders was standing, looking down on all of us grafting away beneath. Then he shouted to us to run up this bloody mountain. Well, I could run for fun and couldn't resist taking the piss out of him. I spotted an ice-cream van and bought the biggest 99 cornet they had. I carried it carefully on the run up and as I reached Saunders I took a big bite out of the flake.

'Have you not got anything harder for me to do?' I asked him. 'This is too easy.'

You should have seen his face. I had taken the mickey out of him literally and he didn't like it one bit.

He didn't see the funny side, either, when I was late for training one day. I had a puncture on the drive from Colwyn Bay doing 90 mph and I was pretty shaken up. I knew he wouldn't believe me, and when I arrived at the training ground I was told he was in a meeting. Well, I opened the boot of my car, lifted out the punctured tyre with my filthy hands and marched to his office. I opened the door and threw the wheel at him and his staff.

'That's why I'm fucking late,' I shouted. If looks could kill. I was lucky he didn't flatten me the same as the tyre.

I wasn't about to last too long at West Brom, then. But I decided to make the most of it while I was there. Although I did feel sorry for the chairman when he called me into his office. I had been staying some nights at a hotel, naturally paid for by the club, and the bar bills were quite excessive. He said, 'I don't mind you spending £750 on champagne as long as I'm involved, Mickey. You have got to book out of the hotel – we can't afford to keep you there.'

I hadn't seen anything wrong with living the high life. I entertained all the players, too. They all put their drinks on my tab. No wonder I was so popular. 'Put it on my bill, Mickey' I was called. The chairman didn't take too kindly to my wild booze sprees but he never got mad with me. I was still his son's favourite player and I knew he was embarrassed that I wasn't being played.

Saunders tried to fix me up with a couple of late moves but every time he phoned I slammed the phone down on him.

I was about to do the same when the phone rang at home until the voice said, 'Mickey, can we have a chat?' It was the manager of Derby County, Arthur Cox. He loved me. And after being rejected by Saunders, I was about to accept a lifeline from a manager I respected.

Arthur wanted to meet me in Stoke for some reason and so I agreed. He talked about a deal – one of the best in my life, by the way.

'You can have a car,' he added. 'All expenses paid, and we'll put you up in the best hotel. We'll give you a hefty bonus for going up, too. Will you come?'

Eleven

Arthur Cox mithered me endlessly to join him at the Baseball Ground. He was a very persistent guy and another manager I signed for because of mutual respect. Derby were already guaranteed promotion, so I wasn't really sure why he was in such a hurry to sign me. I wasn't that keen, I must admit, but what the hell, life in Derby would be a lot happier than life with Sourpuss back at West Brom.

So I signed on another dotted line. I was wanted again – and boy was that a good feeling after all that unrest and upset at The Hawthorns. I couldn't wait to pull on that famous Derby white shirt. Little did I know I was about to start out on a miserable adventure that lasted just nine games.

My first was against Newport County and I was ready to go. Eager, in fact. Perhaps too eager. I was in the warm-up area, kicking the ball against a wall and suddenly . . . ouch. I'd pulled a thigh muscle. Christ, I hadn't even kicked a ball for my new club and I was crocked in the bloody warm-up. But I couldn't let Derby down and so I decided to keep quiet. Not easy for someone with a loose tongue like me.

We went on to win the game and I got away with it. I wasn't my usual fit self, though, and I played in the next game and the one after that. I knew deep down I was struggling. It was a nightmare, to be honest. I wanted to give Derby everything but they were the only club I didn't do well at. I thought I'd got away with it, fooling everyone except myself, until Arthur called me into his office after training one day.

'Mickey,' he said, 'I have watched and admired you throughout your career and you are a super-fit guy. But you seem to be struggling for fitness. What the bloody hell is wrong?'

I didn't want to tell him about my thigh injury. 'To be honest, Gaffer,' I replied, 'it's that fucking Baseball Ground pitch. It's too heavy.'

Arthur, fully aware of how notorious the surface was, agreed that the pitch was to blame. He obviously fell for the bullshit and I played on, in a manner of speaking. I wasn't happy. Fuck it, I thought, I'm not being fair either to Derby or to myself. So I sodded off back to West Brom.

I'd barely got through the door of my hotel when Arthur phoned to ask where the hell I was. I didn't want to hurt the guy but I told him I wasn't going back.

I didn't hear anything more until the end of the season when Derby won that promotion – and a cheque covering my signing-on fee dropped through the letter box at home. I didn't deserve it, but for the first time in my life I decided not to look a gift horse in the mouth.

I still regret to this day, though, the fact that I played the whole time injured. I let everyone there down. But you never leave a place without fond memories – and meeting people you will come across in later life.

Take Steve McClaren. He was at Derby at the same time as me. I used to take Steve and some of the other lads back to my hotel after training. He was officially a Derby player then – but I didn't see much evidence of it. Steve didn't get much of a look-in and you sensed then he was never going to make it in the big time – a bit like the England job really. He didn't really play that much and I definitely couldn't see anything in him then to suggest he would become the manager of England. That was about as likely as Ron Saunders breaking into a smile.

In fact, Steve was so innocuous that I can't recall much about him. Except that he enjoyed my hotel hospitality of free drink and food. No wonder he remembered me years later when I phoned him up to get a signed shirt. He was a coach at Derby at that time and he said, 'I remember you used to look after me, Mickey.'

But while Steve didn't impress me much in my whirlwind Derby stay, my boss Arthur Cox certainly did. He was great to me and had everything in his locker to go onto greater things. An England manager? You bet. He had the appetite and hunger to be successful. A real football man – one of the greats of the game from the old school. Steve McClaren couldn't have had a better manager to learn from on his road to what later proved a disaster for England.

And talking of managers, who should have been the country's choice for the top job in football? Brian Clough. What a bloody disgrace he was never appointed by FA officials, who were never brave enough to give him the role in life he deserved.

His great aura was always around the Baseball Ground. He was the biggest legend Derby ever had. I first came across him when I played for Stoke and he was manager of Nottingham Forest. His son Nigel was loitering on the halfway line and I decided to make my presence known. Whack. I clattered him well and truly. Brian went mad, jumped off the bench and screamed at the referee to book me. For a rare time in his life he was wrong – it should have been a red card.

Some years later we met once again at a charity dinner in Nottingham. Ron Atkinson was on the top table along with Trevor Francis, and I was there to receive an award on behalf of Roy Keane because of my Manchester United connections. I stood up and thanked Brian for bringing a great player like Roy over to England from Cork.

Cloughie immediately got to his feet and gave a speech about me. I couldn't believe it. He said, 'I wasn't going to give a speech tonight. But I think you deserve one.' With that, he praised this little Welsh dragon who had kicked the shit out of his son. Now he was a man. I would have loved to have played for Ol' Big Ed, but I don't think I would have lasted long in his company with our temperaments.

He was a character who most times hated chairmen and always put them in their place. It was a pity no one at Derby could do the same to the Maxwell family when they took control of the club.

One day one of them – I couldn't tell you which one it was because they all looked as though they didn't belong – came up to me and said, 'You're doing really well.' What did he know? I was playing with an injury.

The Maxwells were the forerunners of the big-money owners who have invaded our game today. Nothing changes then. We still have powerful owners of our historic sides who are fully paid-up members of the Know Fuck All Club.

As I said before, I couldn't wait to get away from Derby. I was on a real downer, and not for the usual reasons of pressure, women or drink. It suddenly dawned on me that maybe I was reaching the end of my amazing career. I was pissed off. I had no future at Derby. And no future back at West Brom, where Ron Saunders hadn't made my life easy. He came in with his 'I'm this, I'm that' attitude, the powerful image that he had which just made me disillusioned as I'm a happy-go-lucky guy.

My application had been fantastic to West Brom. He couldn't knock me for my commitment. He was the one in the wrong for not playing me but I was the one on the way out. I was determined, though, to have one last meeting with Saunders. I wanted to tell him finally what I thought, to iron out some problems. That momentous meeting came in the staff car park after training.

'Saunders,' I said. 'I think you *are* a joke.' I was careful to guard my crown jewels but he just smirked and drove off in his flash BMW.

I was fuming. I had a reputation for being mad. A nutter. Uncontrollable. But I always had managers who wanted to sign me and play me. Saunders obviously didn't feel anything for Mickey Thomas. He couldn't handle me, control me. He probably didn't try. And as he drove out of sight I knew that's where I had to be. Far, far away. I didn't reckon on it being that far away, though.

I never ever wanted to move from Colwyn Bay. Now here I was on my way to the United States. God Save America . . .

Twelve

Let's face it, Ron Saunders couldn't have given a stuff about where I ended up after West Brom decided to sell me – providing it was miles away from The Hawthorns.

Well, my next club couldn't have been much further away from the Midlands.

Saunders had given Wichita Wings, an American indoor soccer club based in Kansas, permission to talk to me. The deal had been set up by former Republic of Ireland manager Eoin Hand and it involved Charlie Cooke, the former Chelsea winger and manager of the club, coming to Colwyn Bay to talk to me.

Charlie, a fantastic player in his own right, wanted to come over and assess my physical condition. He didn't have any problems over my skills. He took one look at me and knew I was in good shape and so Wichita bought me and I immediately became one of the first costly transfers for the indoor league in the USA.

At the time, indoor soccer was much bigger than the outdoor version. It was really taking off and attracting fairly decent crowds, especially for the USA. We would regularly sell out our 10,000-capacity stadium.

So there I was, on my way to the other side of the world. There would be no going home every day like I used to during my time at Chelsea. So knowing my track record for my home comforts, what the hell was I doing travelling across the Atlantic?

Strangely, as soon as I got off the plane at Kansas I felt quite at home. It was also nice being in America because no one knew who I was. It was a completely fresh start.

I took my kids over with me. We were all starting a new life. Aaron and Jade naturally went to an American school. That was a whole new experience for them – and for me. At our new home Stateside, there were just the three of us – and I loved that period in my life.

I had no shortage of offers to babysit. The other players' wives were happy to look after the kids whenever I wanted. And that was mostly when we were off on those long flights across that amazing country for away games.

And I was like a kiddy in a sweet shop, too. I enjoyed my football. I had plenty of cash, and precious little of the pressure that had been such an unwelcome companion back in England. The only thing was I knew that I wouldn't be playing proper football.

But the decent money I was getting eased any doubts about the standard of the game. The smiles on the faces of my children helped, too. Playing, though, was full of frustrations. Part of my game was being aggressive, but in indoor soccer you weren't allowed to touch anyone. Physical contact was kept to a minimum. I quickly found this out to my cost as I was constantly sin-binned or even sent off.

The huge distances between the competing clubs meant a lot of jumping on and off planes, and I really couldn't handle the flying bit. I would break out in a sweat just at the thought of being in a plane.

Well, for the Kansas episode of my life to work I needed to conquer my aversion to flying. Luckily, the gaffer, Charlie Cooke was very understanding so he allowed me to get drunk before getting on the plane, which helped settle the nerves.

I think Paul Gascoigne who shared my fear of flying has always followed the 'let's get drunk philosophy' to try and get around the fear.

A couple of times I was hardly able to get off the plane because I was so pissed, but as long as I was on board, the gaffer didn't mind.

One thing I couldn't get my head around, though, was the style of football in the indoor league. There was simply no physical contact, which is complete rubbish in my view. I lost it in a game in Vancouver. Once again I got sent off and we actually lost the game when they scored from the free kick I had given away before being dismissed from the pitch.

In the dressing room I was sitting head down when Charlie Cooke came in and had a go at me for being sent off again. I shouted back that if it was a proper game of football nothing like this would have happened. The American players just looked at me, wondering what I meant. They wouldn't have lasted a minute in the football I knew – by comparison this was a game for namby-pambies.

In the end, it just got to me. I had to leave, but it was a good source of income for two years. Maybe I was the David Beckham of the eighties, blazing a trail in the USA but with no Posh alongside me!

Even though I enjoyed my time in America, I always missed the buzz of what was going on in the UK. Often, to try to keep in touch and find out the football results, myself and another Brit was who was playing for Wichita, the goalkeeper Seamus McDonagh, would be wrestling with the transistor radio, trying to find an English station which would have a commentary or the scores. You always felt that you were missing out on something, even though the American way of life was hugely enjoyable.

There was no pressure on me. The supporters were more interested in munching their popcorn or stuffing hamburgers into their mouths when games were taking place. The biggest thrill for them was when the ball went into the crowd, but why should I care? I was earning good money and safe to say getting to know quite a few American women!

I loved playing for Charlie Cooke as well. He had been a great player and he still took the skills-training, which I enjoyed.

Strangely for someone who always used to get homesick, I barely set foot in the United Kingdom during my two-year exile in the States. One of the few times was for the funeral of my dad who sadly died while I was on the other side of the Atlantic.

My whole world turned upside down when my brother Kev rang to break the news to me that my dad was seriously ill. He had virtually dropped dead in the street with a brain haemorrhage. He didn't have much chance of surviving.

The call came through just before a match and I went on and played the game, but as soon as I arrived back in the dressing room Charlie Cooke told me the news had come through that my dad had passed away. I just broke down in a flood of tears. What was worse, I had this feeling of guilt that I was miles away, unable to help him as he lay there dying.

Going back home was the longest and most distressing journey of my life. I didn't even have a drink to help me get on the plane at Kansas airport. For once, my fear of flying had left me.

I was close to my dad. He had given me my opportunity

to make a name for myself. I should have been there for him, not stuck on the other side of the globe.

We had never been a wealthy family but he always tried to give me the best. He was a steely man himself, who would fight for things in life. He had always given me good advice. The most important was to always show people respect and to give it your best shot all the time. He was very proud of me. In fact, I like to think that the whole family has always been proud of me.

Although I've caused them a few problems along the way, I hope I've also given them much enjoyment. The only thing I can say in my defence when I've slipped off the straight and narrow a few times is that I've never had any real brains to control my life off the pitch – or maybe on it, for that matter.

Today I should have a lot more money than I have, for that same reason. It was just the case that I never ever played for money; I had always wanted to be a footballer. If I had some business acumen maybe I would be a wealthy man right now. But I've always looked after the family financially. And when I was a top player I would give a lot of my wages away. People would look at me in amazement as I went down the street just giving out money to those who didn't have much. It would be a case of handing out £50 here and £50 there. I loved helping people.

There was no need to do that very often in America

because everyone seemed to have enough. Anyway there are more important things in life, as my dad's death proved. At least I had given him some proud moments, like when I made my debut as a player for Wrexham and when I represented my country – he was a very proud Welshman.

While in America I also realised just how far I had come – and also how well a big mate, Mike Peters, the lead singer of the rock group The Alarm, had done. Like me, he had once been an urchin raised on the North Wales coast but I soon came to realise while I was in Kansas that Mike and his group were huge in the USA.

I remember ringing him and telling him that. The Alarm were everywhere; they were big news and were selling loads of records. They were bigger in the USA than back home. I was pleased for Mike especially. He is a super bloke and one I had got to know when I was at Manchester United. He is from Rhyl and I was living there at the time. I loved his music and he loved playing five-a-side football. We would play football together, two ordinary lads from North Wales having made it in our own particular fields.

Mike has since fought off cancer to prove that he is a real fighter as well. I bumped into him not so long ago at an awards do in Cardiff where he was given a lifetime achievement honour for his contribution to Welsh music. He is a real top man and one of my proudest possessions is a CD in which he introduces one of The Alarm's most famous tunes, '68 Guns' by saying this was for his big mate Mickey Thomas. Fantastic. Sometimes you have to pinch yourself about how your life has gone.

But as for the USA and indoor soccer, my time had come and gone. I was ready to say goodbye to it. After two years I had had enough, but now at the age of thirty-four I wondered whether anyone back home would be prepared to – in the words of a big Alarm song – Rescue Me.

Luckily, there had been stories in English papers saying I had become restless in the States. Ian McNeill, who had been John Neal's number two during our days at Chelsea, noticed them and got in touch. He was now in charge of Shrewsbury Town.

My prayers had been answered because I was desperate not to finish my career in the USA, miles away from home.

Ian still had belief in me but wanted to take a look at me in a training session. After just one session I signed for Shrewsbury. I was back!

As for America, I'm afraid football, or soccer as it's known there, will never really take off. Better players than David Beckham, top stars like Pele and Bobby Moore, have tried and failed to help it assume any real importance. The country is too vast and there are too many established American sports competing with football. More youngsters are playing it so all is not lost.

But at the age of thirty-four when I left Kansas it was a case of give me good old Shrewsbury any time!

Thirteen

Still, that flight from America to an English football homecoming was one filled with self-doubt and, to some extent, fear. After all, I was two years older than when I had last played in this country.

The thing I was clinging to – hopefully the attribute that was going to save me – was my fitness. I've always kept myself supremely fit, even to this day. But there was still a fog of doubt whirling around me, and so thank goodness for the words of an airport worker shortly after we landed at Manchester.

Immediately after getting off the plane this guy shouts out 'Mickey Thomas – Manchester United.' Fantastic, I thought, I haven't been forgotten, after all.

All I had to do now was to convince the Shrewsbury manager, Ian McNeill, that I hadn't forgotten how to play football at a decent level. He had invited me for a training session because, to be fair to him, he didn't know what two years of indoor football in the USA had done to me. Thankfully, straight after the training session he told me that he wanted to sign me. I even received a signing-on fee – nothing extortionate, but very welcome, all the same.

At that time Shrewsbury were punching above their weight in the old Second Division, the second tier of football. There were some big sides in that division as well: the likes of Chelsea, Leeds United and Manchester City. In any case, I was so desperate to play again in the Football League that I couldn't have cared less what level I was performing.

There was still, though, some local rivalry to contend with before I had even kicked a ball for Shrewsbury. The fact that I had started my career just across the border at Wrexham hadn't gone down too well for some people, including, it seemed, the local Shrewsbury press.

One of the early headlines that greeted me was: 'HE MIGHT NOT SET THE PITCH ALIGHT BUT HE WILL SOON LIGHT UP THE NIGHTLIFE!' I thought, Thanks very much you bastards . . .

That made me determined to prove them wrong and in many ways these detractors inspired me. Not that there was much inspiration in being stuck up in the Scottish wilds of Aberdeen as part of the pre-season build up. There was no palatial hotel to act as a base. Instead, we were all booked into a hostel more suited to backpackers than professional footballers. There was no chance of misbehaving; the nearest place of any interest was an oil rig out in the North Sea! I didn't fancy swimming out to that . . .

I must have started to become boring in my old age because the thing that kept me going was extra training with Les Helm, the physio. Les was a real straight guy, someone you couldn't mess with. He was impressed with my fitness. After everyone else had finished we would go off running. It was great for me, just what I needed as I prepared for my first season back after the American adventure.

My first game for Shrewsbury was at home to Portsmouth and although we ended up losing 2–1, I was named Man of the Match, and that helped win over some of those fans who had given me stick because of my Wrexham connections.

I ended up playing in forty of the forty-six league games and really enjoyed myself in what was to become an inevitable battle to avoid relegation.

In my first away game, George Courtney, then one of the top referees, was in charge. I was in the tunnel before the game when George came over and asked whether he could grab my autograph after the game for his wife.

That was no problem. About twenty minutes into the game I received a right old whack. George hovered over me as I lay on the ground and said, 'Welcome back to the Football League, Mickey.'

I asked him if I could repay the compliment to the sod who had just kicked me. George said no, I couldn't.

So I just said, 'Right then, I won't sign your autograph book!'

It was a tough season, because we never got out of the relegation zone but Shrewsbury's plight never got to me. I felt I conducted myself well on and off the pitch.

In fact, David Moyes, who has gone on to manage Everton but who was just making his way as a central defender at Shrewsbury, later described me as the perfect professional, super fit and a top guy.

Now at long last I can repay the compliment because little did David know at the time but I was considering appointing him as my number two if I moved into management.

Mickey Thomas, manager! Yes, I know some of you will be killing yourself with laughter at that one – but it very nearly happened. With Shrewsbury struggling the writing appeared to be on the wall for the manager Ian McNeill. I was popular at Gay Meadow – hell, what a name for a football ground – and I won pretty well every Player of the Year award that was going.

One day I was told by the chairman that the board saw me as the club's next manager. Although it was very tempting, I felt loyalty to Ian McNeill who had given me my chance at Shrewsbury. If it had come to the crunch I would have turned the job down but it didn't stop me considering what I would do if I stepped into management.

And I would definitely have picked David Moyes as

my assistant. He was much younger than me, but a tremendously determined character. I remember him playing in one game with a broken nose. I thought at the time, He'll do for me.

Moysey is the sort of person you would want in the trenches with you and it's no surprise that he has gone on to become one of the top managers in the country. We might be like chalk and cheese but I felt we would have complemented each other. I also liked him as a person, and as a player he was as brave as a lion. He was a leader in the dressing room, even at a relatively young age.

Deep down, though, I wanted to continue playing. After all it's what I loved doing. Football management would have to wait, and there was no way I was going to step into Ian McNeill's shoes after the loyalty he had shown me.

But it was a great compliment. Here was a club believing I could manage them when many people thought I couldn't even manage myself! Playing for Shrewsbury was certainly different to what I had been used to. For a start, you would only attract crowds of around 5,000 for home games. In fact, I'm sure they used to name the crowd before they named the team at Gay Meadow!

You just had to get on with it. Instead of a sea of faces, which would surround you at the big grounds like Old Trafford and Stamford Bridge, you would notice individuals. You could also hear every word uttered. I would always be singled out for terrible stick from the opposition fans because I was the 'name' in the Shrewsbury team.

During one match I was preparing to take a corner when one of the local coppers told to me how much he admired me for putting up with it. Well, there wasn't any real alternative, was there? And in many ways I enjoyed it. It always inspired me to try to shove the taunts back down those fans' throats by doing something on the pitch against their team.

Despite our plight, I gave everything for Shrewsbury Town. I was back in the limelight because there were some big games in the division against Leeds United, Blackburn, Manchester City and my old club, Chelsea.

When Shrewsbury first came calling I had feared they just needed a new coracle man. Many of you will remember that Gay Meadow was situated right next to the River Severn and so the club had to employ a bloke who would row out to collect any stray balls that landed in the river in his little coracle! No, I was out there in front of smaller crowds to be fair, but still doing the business as a footballer.

Our last home game of the season was against Leeds United, which ended up as a 3–3 draw. After the game, I had to return to the dressing room because I had forgotten my bag. As I was coming out into the corridor next to the dressing rooms, the Leeds assistant manager

Mick Hennigan called out, 'Mickey, can you give us a ring at Elland Road on Monday?'

I told him I would, no problem. I thought I knew what it was all about: one of our players, Bernard McNally, who was more than decent, had warmed up before the game with a 'For Sale' notice strapped to his back. It was done as a joke but he did want to try and move on and to better himself.

When I returned to the players' lounge I told Bernard to give me his telephone number because I thought that Mick Hennigan would be asking me all about Bernard when I called him on Monday.

You can imagine my surprise when I made that call and things turned out very differently.

Fourteen

My phone call that Monday was answered by Howard Wilkinson. 'How do you fancy playing for Leeds?' he said in that slow, serious voice of his.

I lightened the tone immediately. 'You can fuck off,' I replied. 'You slaughtered me in my Chelsea days. You said I would sod off and fall out with the boss. You did me in.'

Imagine my surprise, then, when he told me he had admired me all through my career. 'It's an opportunity for me to finally sign you,' he said. 'I want you to sign for Leeds United. We're building for the future here and I want you to be a big part of it. You are the type of player we want at Elland Road.'

So I went back across to Yorkshire and met Howard, who introduced me to his chairman Bill Fotherby at the stadium. I did a deal straight away. Yes, signed another contract. I should have gone there for nothing but Shrewsbury wanted £10,000. That money should have been mine but, as usual, I didn't get a penny. But, hey, what the hell? I was a Leeds United player. Or was I?

Pre-season hadn't even started when I got a phone call out of the blue from Norman Wilson, the secretary at Tranmere who was with me at Wrexham during the early part of my career.

'Why don't you come and sign for Tranmere, Mickey?' he said. 'It will be nearer for you than driving across the Pennines to Leeds.'

I told him I had signed for Leeds but he was having none of it. He explained that technically I could still get out of the deal and asked me to go and meet him at the club. Then I got another phone call, this time from the daughter of the manager, Johnnie King, asking me over as well. I could never resist an invitation from a woman – still can't – so I made the trip. I took along my Leeds contract, thinking that maybe I didn't fancy a two-hour journey to Yorkshire every day.

I showed it to my mate, the Tranmere secretary. I didn't think there was any harm in it. I knew him well. This meeting was discreet, I thought. Norman studied the contract in detail before declaring that Tranmere couldn't match any of the terms. So with a handshake I was off and heading for my new life at Elland Road.

Two days later I got another phone call, this time to herald my worst ever start to a new career. Mick Hennigan was on the other end of the line. 'Mickey son, we have a problem,' he told me. 'We're not very happy with you. You have been talking with Tranmere. We know all about it.'

Shit. I had only gone to see Tranmere as a favour to Norman and now I'd been rumbled, dropped in it from a bloody great height. I was disappointed that someone at Tranmere had blabbed about the meeting but luckily nothing serious came of it.

So with that nonsense behind me, I couldn't wait to start pre-season training and link up with my new team-mates. And what a squad Howard had assembled for the start of the 1989 season, which was to see Leeds finish as Second Division champions. Look at this for a line-up of stars: Vinnie Jones, Gordon Strachan and John Hendrie were already there. Leeds also had Lee Chapman, Chris Fairclough, Bobby Davison, Ian Baird, Mel Sterland, Mervyn Day, David Batty.

We had some characters – and some hard men. I remember the local paper running an article which posed the question: which player would get booked first – Vinnie, Batts, Ian Baird or me? Our first game was a meaningless friendly and, yes, you've guessed it, I claimed the prize. Vinnie, though, was a wonderful guy. A great lad. Top drawer. He knew his limitations – Howard made sure of that.

In one training session, Vinnie tried to do a bit of skill, which was like trying to get a show pony to jump Bechers. Well, Howard saw what he was doing and immediately stopped the game and shouted, 'What are you doing, Vinnie? Leave the skill to Mickey Thomas and Gordon Strachan.'

With everyone falling about laughing, Mick Ennigun piped up, 'We only bought you to take the throw-ins.'

Vinnie took the banter in his stride and was great to have around in the dressing room. He was full of life and a brilliant personality. So loveable, really.

People always got the wrong impression of him. They thought he was a horrible guy – and on the pitch he could be at times. But he would give you anything. He used to have a bet with Batts and Strach on how long I would sit down for because I was always hyper. Vinnie was like me in many ways: he loved the game with a passion. His many critics said he didn't have ability but I watched him closely and he wasn't bad.

I'll never forget him coming to my testimonial after all those years. I made a phone call and he flew up with his minder. He paid all his own hotel and travelling expenses. Everything. I really admire him for that. Vinnie is a man of his word. I have an amazing amount of time for him. I never imagined that one day he would be a film star living in Los Angeles. If he's looking for a co-star I'm his man. Never mind *Bend It Like Beckham*. I'm more a *Make 'Em Like Mickey*.

We had a ball in our short spell together at Leeds. My Elland Road career was to be cruelly restricted by injury – the first serious problem, not of my own making, in life. I developed cartilage trouble and I had an operation ten days before the start of that first season. I worked my bollocks off after keyhole surgery and got fit for the opening game against Newcastle at St James' Park.

I wore the number-four shirt that day and Vinnie was on the bench. We were winning 2–1 and I had a chance to increase that to 3–1. The ball came across the eighteen-yard box and instead of stopping I tried to hit the ball first time with my trusty left boot. I missed the target. Bollocks. We ended up losing 5–2, with Mickey Quinn scoring a hat trick. I wasn't happy and before the final whistle I went in for a tackle and came off the worst. Christ, I had done my knee in again.

The same bloody knee. I carried on regardless, though, and we played Middlesbrough on the Wednesday in what was to be Gary Pallister's last game before he joined my old club, Manchester United. I ended up going in for a 50–50 with Gary and felt that old familiar twinge in the knee. I came off again for Vinnie and we ended up winning 2–1. You can't keep a good little 'un down, though, and I was in the team for the following Saturday's game against Blackburn.

I knew I was struggling. I started the game but had to come off, and Vinnie got off the bench and did the honours again. I'd had enough of the creasing pain now and at training on the Monday I told Howard that I needed another operation. It took a while to get myself fit after that, and my life was never the same at Leeds after that. I think what happened at Tranmere still played on the manager's mind. And I don't think I did myself any favours, either, by trying to help out Noel Blake.

He was having problems and wanted to do an article in the *News of the World*. I knew someone on the paper and told Noel I would give him the reporter's number. He rang, the story appeared, and I think Howard blamed me. Next thing I was fit but in the reserves against Liverpool at Elland Road.

I scored a rocket of a goal into the top corner. It was a great goal, even though I say it myself. Anyway, half-time came and Mick Hennigan told me I was coming off.

Jim Beglin, sitting next to me, said, 'You're probably straight back into the first team on Saturday, Mickey.'

Well, I waited for the call-up. Nothing came. I didn't know what was going on. I was fit, bursting to play. But instead of opening my gob again I decided to keep my head down. That bastard knee went again, though, and I faced a third operation. I was so used to the procedure by now I could have picked up the scalpel and repaired the damage myself. Three operations in six months. What a load of crap. I never gave up, though, and got myself back into shape. But what made it harder to get back was that Leeds were flying by now. Gary Speed, who would become another great Welsh hero, was on the verge of getting into the team. Leeds were really buzzing.

The only downside was that Batts wasn't happy. He had a massive dilemma over whether he should stay or go from Elland Road. He was in and out of the team. His head was in bits, so why he should turn to me for advice God only knows. He did. And he said later in a magazine interview that it was the best bit of advice he'd ever had in his life. From Mickey T.

Batts asked me, 'What do you think I should do? Do you think I should leave?'

I told him not to go. 'Leeds are a big club,' I said. 'I think you should stay. Perservere and you will get back into the side. You will be fine. Mark my words. You don't know how it will turn out at another club. Trust me. I have had the experience of that.'

Well, he took my words of wisdom and stayed. The rest is history, as Batts became a great player for Leeds and an England international. Christ. With my skills I should have been a lawyer – and not later employing one.

While Batts had shown his frustration on the sidelines, I had my own problems with not being a regular. The opportunities never came my way again. The distractions away from the pitch kept my spirits up, though. I used to travel a lot with Jim Beglin and we became regulars at a Leeds snooker club run by former World Champion Joe Johnson. One night Jim told me that this blonde bird fancied me but I didn't want to know. I wasn't interested. Help, call for the medics, I must be ill.

Anyway, she gave me her phone number but I never called her. So she started ringing me at the club. Then this blonde beaut bombarded me with pictures of herself, raunchy ones at that, too. Naked. Wow. What I didn't know was the trouble those nude photographs would land another Leeds player in.

It happened after I was speaking one day to one of the lads who had just moved into a new home. I had asked him for his telephone number and scribbled it on the back of an envelope with those dirty pictures of the blonde inside. As usual, in a dizzy moment, I left the envelope and number – and photos – in the dressing room and completely forgot about everything.

Until four or five days later when this lad came up to me, looking worried. He said: 'I'm going to have to call the police in. Someone is making dirty phone calls to my missus.'

I didn't twig at first. Then I looked behind this lad to see another Leeds player – who I'll not name and shame – shaking his head. It turned out he had found the envelope with the porno pictures and phone number and thought he'd give the blonde a ring. Oops, wrong number, I do believe. Sorry.

Anyway, back to football. Or should I say lack of football. I was basically just killing time at Elland Road. The team, unlike me, were doing great. I kept telling everyone I was fit to play but no one listened. I just played now and again for the reserves. I travelled a lot for not much satisfaction and I was late a lot, too. I don't know whether Howard felt sorry for me or not but he never fined me. Didn't talk to me, either. So I decided to break my rare vow of silence and confront him. Why it had taken so long I don't know. I was blunt as usual.

'Are you going to play me?' I said. But he didn't really give me an answer, just told me to keep myself fit. I knew, though, he didn't want me in the team.

I couldn't help but like him, though. Everyone else at Leeds had lived in fear of him. I remember Vince Hilaire used to hide when he saw Howard coming down the corridor. Howard was a very powerful man. But I used to go up to him, pat him on the back, and say: 'Hi, Gaffer. How was your night last night? Did you get a shag?'

He loved me. He was a tough man, though, and quite rightly deserved the reputation as a disciplinarian. Sgt Wilko was about right.

After one defeat, he gathered all the club professionals into the dressing room, even those who hadn't played.

'Right, you lot,' he barked, 'you are in tomorrow. It's Sunday and you are coming in for extra training.'

I wasn't having that, and I walked out and told Mick Hennigan I was going back to good old Colwyn Bay to be with my kids.

'Well, you tell him, I'm not going to,' he said.

Don't you worry. I wasn't afraid of Wilko. I found him in the referee's room getting changed. I went in and said, 'Hey, I'm not coming in tomorrow. You might be bringing that lot in on a Sunday but I won't be there.'

He just shrugged and never fined me for my rebel-rousing. I wouldn't have coughed up anyway. My time at Elland Road was coming to an abrupt end.

I was there eighteen months. Played those three games and suffered those three operations. But do you know, I never regretted going there. Remember I had gone there as a kid and struggled with the rejection. At least I had finally made it as a Leeds player all those eventful years later. It took a long and winding road but I had got there in the end.

Time was called after a phone call from Alan Ball, and a return to Stoke was next stop. I don't suppose I really had to go. But you know me, I wanted to play. Professionals these days are quite content to park their arses on the substitutes' bench and pick up their big fat wage packets. Hanging around as a bit-part player wasn't my idea of football life. I still wanted to play every game. I didn't give a damn about anything else.

That ball really was my lover. And I desperately wanted to be with it again. I still think about what would have happened if I had stuck it out at Leeds. I could have been in their Championship-winning side. But that's the story of my career. If I hadn't have got itchy feet then great things could have happened in my life. If I had stayed at Manchester United; stayed at Chelsea . . . But I was my own person.

I wasn't in any mood to feel part of the Leeds celebrations at the end of that first season. I'm a proud man and was missing again when the team boarded the open-topped bus for the champagne trip around the city. I didn't want to be part of that – unless they had asked me to be the driver. I didn't even get a medal. I didn't deserve one, I suppose, after playing just three games. I wouldn't have taken it if it had been offered anyway.

The team earned the success. I didn't. But there were no hard feelings and certainly no bad vibes directed at Howard. He had put me back in the spotlight and given me the chance of another go at the big time at thirty-six years of age. That wasn't bad, was it? Although it could have gone better at Leeds if I had stayed free of injuries – and stayed away from Tranmere.

Looking back, and I seldom do, I have got so much time for Howard even to this day. The last English manager to win the title. That says it all really.

Fifteen

Alan Ball was one of my heroes as a football-crazy youngster and the fact that he wanted to sign me gave me a huge buzz. He was a great player – England international, World Cup winner. It doesn't get much better than that, does it?

He was so passionate about the game, something which would shine through in the time I played under him. So a return to Stoke City, the club that Bally now managed, was a no-brainer, especially after I had enjoyed it so much the first time around eight years earlier.

When he came calling I couldn't sign quick enough. I knew the Stoke fans would welcome me back with open arms because I had enjoyed a great rapport with them. And don't forget I used to drink with some of them, those hard nuts who called themselves 'the Naughty Forties'. Stoke had a great fan base; they really took football seriously in the Potteries. It was my kind of place.

I knew that Alan wanted sides to replicate his brand of football. He was hot-headed as a player and wanted sides with energy. But most of all he wanted to win. Funnily enough, the thing that had first attracted me to him as a starry-eyed kid was the fact that he wore white boots – unheard of in his era.

Add his red hair and he really stood out. He was tenacious, a wonderful player. Some people have told me that I had the same energy levels as a player – compliments don't come much bigger or better than that.

Sadly it was to prove a fairly unhappy time for Alan Ball at Stoke. In fact, he didn't really have too successful a time as a manager wherever he went. He was probably too honest for his own good. He would see things going on out on the pitch that he didn't like and would want to change it straight away. You can't always do that because the players aren't good enough. That meant he was aggressive in the dressing room. Quite simply, most of the players he was in charge of couldn't reach the heights that he was capable of as a player and so there would be confrontations. He spoke from the heart and could be very hard on some players. He was explosive and said what he felt.

I will always remember the looks of shock on all our faces after one bizarre incident on a Monday at the training ground. On the previous Saturday it had been widely reported in the press and on the television that

Neville Southall, the Wales goalkeeper, had been involved in a huge bust-up with his Everton manager, Colin Harvey. Now don't forget Harvey was a member of that magnificent Everton misfield of the sixties: Harvey, Ball and Howard Kendall.

Anyway, it ended up with Neville, always his own man, staging a protest against Harvey by coming out at half-time and sitting with his back against one of the goalposts.

All this had obviously badly affected Alan Ball. He believed it was an affront to all managers, not just his big mate Harvey. So although none of us had been within a million miles of the Goodison Park flashpoint, Bally believed he should make a stand for all managers against rebellious players.

He entered the changing room as we prepared for our normal Monday training session and shouted out, 'You lot can train on your fucking own today. That Neville Southall is a disgrace.'

With that he just walked out and wasn't seen for the rest of the day, leaving the training to his assistant Graham Paddon. But that was Alan Ball. He felt a sense of solidarity to Colin Harvey and thought that, for twenty-four hours at least, all players were a disgrace.

To say we were left in a state of shock is an understatement but Alan Ball didn't take any prisoners. I still enjoyed playing for him – and, in any case, I was all right because I was his type of player. Like Bally in his heyday I could run for ever, always having boundless energy.

But when Stoke sacked him I suppose I became vulnerable. I still managed to win some awards but that didn't save me in the end. If Bally had been around I don't think he would have stood for what happened to me at the end of the season.

Graham Paddon had become the caretaker manager but he didn't have any power because it was only a matter of time before Stoke brought in somebody else. I don't know to this day the reasons why Stoke cooled on me. Maybe they didn't like some of the types I was hanging around with. Maybe it wasn't the done thing to share drinks with members of 'the Naughty Forties'. It hadn't bothered anyone the first time around at the club.

Anyway, one day I received a call from a girl from the ground, Diane. I could tell by her voice that she was panicking and felt uneasy about ringing me. I asked her what the matter was. She said that she was calling to tell me that the club were releasing me. She said it was Graham Paddon's decision.

I told her that was a load of bollocks because he was on the way out himself. I asked her whether it was the decision of the chairman, Peter Coates.

Well, it turned out that it was down to him. Why? I honestly don't know. I also felt it was grossly unfair because I had done the business on the pitch. But this was now a serious matter. I was getting on in years, well into my mid-thirties. Where was I going to go? I had been banking on another season at Stoke.

For the first time in my life I felt as though I was in a vacuum, with nothing on the horizon. It was the summer, I was out of work and with no real prospects. I don't suppose I could really have complained if that had been the end of my playing. I'd had some life as a footballer, even if I didn't have the money to go with it.

As I've told you before, I was never financially sound – I'm still not. I never used to think about money. As soon as I got it in my hands I spent it. I wasn't intelligent when it came to money. Come to think of it, I've never been intelligent full stop!

Now, though, for me it was a severe reality check. It was a few weeks of hell, there's no doubt about that. Here I was, back home in Colwyn Bay, back to where it all started. I was even back running on the beach and in the Welsh mountains to try to retain my fitness.

When you are young you think that the good times are going to last for ever. Bang! With a jolt, I was back down to earth, with my arse hanging out of my pants. What did the future hold? Where were all those people I knew when I was playing for Manchester United, Everton and Chelsea?

Then I had always been surrounded by so-called friends. But as you get older, and don't have the same fame value, you are quickly discarded. It's a cruel fact of life.

But I've always been a fighter. Yes, I was in the last-chance saloon but in my mind last orders still hadn't been called. But if no football club came in for me, what was I going to do to try to eke out a living?

I didn't have any other talents, just the ability to kick a ball around a football field. There was no brain, just a footballing brain. My head was almost busting. Why hadn't I been sensible and put some money away for a rainy day? Suddenly it was pouring and I was in the shit. I didn't have an agent. The only agents I knew were the newsagents!

Thankfully, all my prayers were answered when my old club Wrexham came in for me. They couldn't sign me straight away because they couldn't afford to pay me in the summer without any revenue from games. They were hard up, just like me. The fact that they wanted me and would sign me just before the start of the season was music to my ears.

I wasn't a washed-up former professional footballer after all.

Sixteen

When Wrexham said they wanted to sign me I wasn't about to lose my grip on a lifeline. Manager Brian Flynn, who I had known from our days playing for Wales, assured me that the deal was on. But I had an agonising wait over the summer before I could join the club officially all those years after Wrexham had given me my first big break in football.

It was good to be back. My heart had never really been taken out of the club that had first given me the opportunity to become a professional footballer and embark on a journey of discovery – and heartbreak. This time around it was so different, but I thank them again today for giving me the chance to wear the shirt with pride.

The dreams I had had as a kid had been fulfilled. The nightmares, too.

Now I was back at Little Wrexham. I was winding down my career, trying to hang on in there at the ripe old age of thirty-seven. But I was still determined to play at a decent level. I had kicked binge drinking AND pounding the streets and beaches of Colwyn Bay to make sure the old knee joints kept moving.

I was still harbouring a huge disappointment that it had gone so horribly wrong at Stoke because the chairman wanted me out. I knew beggars couldn't be choosers but I didn't have any hesitation in signing again for Wrexham. Give it another go, Mickey, I kept telling myself and I knew, too, that Flynnie was convinced that I could still do it. He could tell that from my first training session. In fact, I left no one in any doubt that I could still perform at that level.

I knew the ability hadn't deserted me. The years had advanced but I certainly didn't feel like a has-been. Far from it. I was ready for the new challenge and my first home game against Hereford couldn't come soon enough. We lost 2–1 but it was a great debut for me and I collected another Man of the Match award. The crowd were brilliant. The prodigal son had returned, back in the red of Wrexham.

It felt good. Fantastic. There were only about 5,000 fans in the Racecourse Ground but it felt like 50,000. They loved me. I loved them. And I had a strong feeling that this young Wrexham team I had joined were beginning their own journey to something special. Just how special I would never have guessed.

We had Gordon Davies, ex-Fulham and Wales striker.

In goal was Vince O'Keefe, a truly great professional. I had a lot of time for Vince. Brian Carey had arrived from Manchester United and we had a young lad up front, Lee Jones. Mark Sertori was a big guy at the back. It was a team full of promise.

The only question was whether Wrexham could keep their talented kids. The team had been struggling and the club was financially in the shit. The years hadn't been kind to the Racecourse Ground. In my absence it had deteriorated alarmingly. There were state-of-the-art grounds springing up all over Britain but this was a throwback to the past. More a state of the ark. They certainly didn't have bundles of spare cash, judging by my first pay packet of just under £300 a week.

I was rich in terms of enjoying my football again, though. Out on the pitch I felt back to my best and the games came thick and fast. The season gained momentum and, in truth, we were doing well, although the financial situation was dragging the club down. Wrexham had less cash in the bank than me.

But then, out of the blue, came our FA Cup run, which began cranking up at places like Winsford United and Telford before that historic third-round draw sealed the club's destiny. I remember watching the draw live on TV and couldn't believe my eyes when Wrexham's ball came out of the bag followed by Arsenal. Bloody Arsenal. The Mighty Gunners. Christ.

All the memories came flooding back of that FA Cup

Final defeat at the hands of Arsenal in my Manchester United days. Now it was time for revenge, although that prospect seemed as likely as Mickey Thomas being elected the Governor of the Bank of England. I've learned in life, though, that nothing is impossible and if you believe, well, you never know. What I couldn't believe was the build-up to the big game on 4 January 1992 at the Racecourse Ground. I had experienced massive games but suddenly everyone wanted a piece of me. I was back in the spotlight and I admit I enjoyed the attention again.

There was a serious side, though, to all the fun and frolics leading up to the tie. The story went around that Flynnie would get the sack after the Arsenal game because the club couldn't afford his wages. They didn't have enough revenue coming in to keep him and were going bust, big style. But along came the game that changed everyone's life at Wrexham for ever.

Wrexham went from strength to strength after that amazing day and Flynnie continued to do a great job for the club, along with my mate Joey and Kevin Reeves. Although we all braced ourselves for another major car crash when the Arsenal team coach arrived ninety minutes before kick-off.

I was there to see this cruise liner pull up outside. They even had their own chef on board and the Arsenal lads looked like a million dollars when they skipped down the steps into the players' entrance. It was like a Who's Who of football: George Graham, the manager; Tony Adams, the skipper; David Seaman, Lee Dixon, Nigel Winterburn, David O'Leary, Paul Merson, David Rocastle. They looked like gladiators entering the arena. Thank goodness Ian Wright was injured.

I was captain on the day and went into the referee's room before the game for our instructions on how to behave. So I was standing there next to Adams and the Gunners' boss, George. They were both immaculately turned out in club suits. I was standing there in a ripped T-shirt and holes in my socks. We looked each other up and down. Rich men, poor man.

I couldn't wait to get back to the dressing room to get stripped and we didn't get much of a team talk. The message from the boss was to give it our best shot. Arsenal came to Wrexham as League Champions. We had finished bottom of the old Fourth Division and only stayed in the Football League by default because someone else's ground wasn't up to standard.

I remember lining up in the tunnel alongside Adams. The *Match of the Day* cameras awaited. So did a packed house. I turned round and shook the Arsenal captain by the hand. I squeezed as hard as I could to leave him with the impression that we were bloody well up for this.

'All the best,' I said. I couldn't think of anything more original to say. I certainly wasn't going to crack any of those Donkey Adams jokes. I had made a twat of myself too many times to wind up this giant of a man.

I got on the pitch. The referee Kevin Breen – from, of all places, Liverpool – blew the first whistle and we were off on the great adventure. We had a monster amount of luck in the first half and they only got the one goal through Alan Smith. But Merson had murdered us for the forty-five minutes.

Half-time came and half-time went. Arsenal had battered us but we were still in the game at 1–0 down. Anything could happen – and it did. The history books of the FA Cup are jammed with massive shock results and Wrexham were about to write another glorious page. We flew out of the blocks in the second half and began to create half chances here and there.

Ten minutes remained when referee Breen awarded us a free kick after O'Leary was penalised for a foul on Gordon Davies about twenty-five yards out. Although I still claim it was thirty yards. A couple of lads fancied having a go. But I said to Wayne Phillips, 'Leave it. I'm hitting this.'

I had smacked a free kick the previous day in training where I didn't take much of a run up and it went in like a rocket.

I decided to use the same technique. Steve Watkin and Gordon were in the wall and I aimed for them spot on. They parted, opened up a gap and the ball flew like a missile into the top corner.

My trusty left boot had summoned up so much power in that dead-ball strike and Seaman didn't stand a chance. He made a despairing save and got a touch. The ball slightly touched his fingertips but bang, it was in the back of the net. We were 1–1 and the place erupted. I ran straight to Joey who was on the bench and jumped all over him. It was one of the best feelings I had ever had in football. At my age I didn't think I could leap that high.

I scored at the end where all the Arsenal fans were standing, and to this day I can still remember all their sad faces. I can also recall vividly an excited Wrexham steward in a yellow jacket running up and down the stairs in the stand. Talk about a contrast in emotions.

I couldn't help thinking about the circumstances of the game. There were Arsenal rolling in money; Wrexham without a bean to their name. One team at the top. The other at the bottom. And I had scored probably the best goal of my career. I gulped for air. Fuck me, this was bloody exciting. I could see the Arsenal boys start to wobble. Suddenly they had fear in their eyes and they blinked in disbelief when we scored the winner within two minutes. Gareth Owen helped on Andy Thackeray's throw-in and Gordon Davies ran it on before playing the ball into the box.

Little Steve Watkin gambled by going near-post and as big Adams slipped, Stevie steered the ball into the far corner for that amazing 2–1 win. That goal – and mine – was flashed around the world and exiled Wrexham fans in Hong Kong, America and Australia went bananas.

But for those 13,343 fans packed inside the Racecourse Ground it was a day to be etched in their memory for the rest of their lives: an 'I was there' moment. I certainly was and the first person I grabbed at the whistle was poor young Merson. He shook my hand and told me well done. It was madness and all the lads were carried around the pitch on the fans' shoulders.

Before the game I had asked David Seaman if I could have his gloves afterwards for my son, Aaron. I thought that was the only thing I would get out of the game. It took me fifteen minutes to get off the pitch through the celebrating crowd and what happened next I will treasure for as long as I live.

There, waiting down the tunnel, by the dressing-room door was Dave. I couldn't believe it. He had just been humiliated in one of the greatest FA Cup upsets of all time. He had been embarrassed and beaten twice by little Welsh minnows. But there he was, still waiting for me with his gloves in his hand.

'These are for your boy,' he said, handing over the memento.

'I can't believe you're still here,' I replied.

'No, I wanted to give the gloves to you,' big Dave added. 'They don't work anyway . . .'

I gave the gloves to Aaron and he came in our dressing room. We danced, hugged, kissed. I don't ever remember snogging so many blokes in my life. It's a good job they didn't know about that in prison.

Wrexham were famous – and Mickey would be treated like a superstar again.

The *Match of the Day* producers asked me to appear that night and a limo arrived to whisk me over to the BBC's Manchester studios. My goal was shown over and over. And I must admit, sixteen years later it still gives me a massive thrill. The interview went well and the end titles rolled. I was driven back home in style but I didn't want the day to end and I managed to make it for last orders at my local, the Queen's Head.

The roar when I walked into the pub was deafening; the handshakes and slaps on the back firm and friendly. I had so many pints of Guinness bought I could have swam in the black stuff.

I was massive news again. On the Richter scale of football shocks you couldn't get a bigger one than that. Emotionally I was drained. But so, so happy. The good times had rolled back at thirty-seven and I felt like a kid starting over at Wrexham the first time around.

I'm sure Dave doesn't like to be reminded about my rocket left footer. And I'm equally certain that he closes his eyes every time the repeat is shown on the telly. But everyone I meet to this day stops me to talk about *that* goal. They remember it, like I do, as though it was yesterday.

I have seen the strike a hundred times and never tire of it. But the goal celebrations weren't just restricted to Wrexham and the Racecourse Ground. I was told afterwards that Chelsea had played Hull that day and when my old fans heard the result they sang my name at full throttle. Tottenham supporters, who despised me for that wink on *Match of the Day*, sent me letters of congratulation.

It was Arsenal's biggest modern-day embarrassment and Chelsea and Spurs fans made the most of it. Loved it. Loved me. The party went on in the Queen's Head until well after midnight but my recollection of the day wasn't clouded by viewing life from the bottom of a Guinness glass.

I clearly remember, too, what a great man George Graham was that day. A man of integrity and honour, despite the hurt of defeat. I have an enormous amount of respect for him. And his players. Arsenal took that defeat on the chin and I don't think Arsene Wenger would have handled himself on the day with the same kind of decorum and humility.

The following morning our famous victory was naturally still big, big news. My mug beamed out from the TV sets from the moment the egg and bacon breakfasts were served up in millions of homes. Little did I know then that less than a week later I would be making the national TV news for a very different reason.

Seventeen

My brother Kev always went out to buy the Sunday papers. The day after that unbelievable win against Arsenal he came back with more than usual.

After all, Wrexham and Mickey Thomas weren't just making the headlines on the back pages, we were all over some of the front pages as well. Sadly, as you already know, it wasn't to be the one and only time that yours truly adorned the front covers of Britain's best-selling publications.

I was feeling on top of the world. Before the Arsenal game I thought that my days of being headline news were long gone. I was in my twilight years, seeing out my career where it had all started – at Wrexham. Now here I was in the aftermath of that wonder goal against the Gunners, doing newspaper articles virtually every day. I was a media star when I least expected it. People who had forgotten my phone number were ringing me again. How life can change.

The win against Arsenal also had a profound effect on Wrexham: the club and the town. Before the Gunners arrived, the club was really struggling. It was badly in need of money and the manager, Brian Flynn, was in danger of the sack. Now with the Arsenal money banked and with the prospect of another big pay day – we had been drawn away to West Ham United in the fourth round – the club was coming out of the doldrums.

In addition, the whole town, which really had been on a downer over the past years, was buzzing again. Wrexham, who had stirred the nation with some of its footballing deeds in previous years, was back in action, sending shock waves everywhere with the Arsenal victory.

I was loving it. Everyone wanted a piece of me again and I had no complaints: I was back in the spotlight, life was grand.

Well, it was until the following weekend! Only a week before the Thomas family had been lapping up the Arsenal-smashing headlines. This Sunday I was watching a game on television without a care in the world when a fearful hammering on my front door turned my life upside down.

This was the day when the police came to arrest me, the day they accused me of being involved in the forging of £10 notes.

I've already described to you earlier in the book about this sullen and frightening day, of how my house was surrounded like a scene from *The Bill*. What I haven't really gone into was the horrible wait – an unacceptable eighteen months – before I was brought to trial. Imagine being kept on tenterhooks for a year and a half on anything: a medical scare, exam results, a job application. It would be torture. Now imagine how I felt with my freedom at stake.

In many ways, the wait and the nervy anticipation were worse than the actual sentence. At least that brought some finality, while before it all kinds of things ran through my head.

But this was the reality: Mickey Thomas, miracle worker against Arsenal, was reduced to a quivering wreck not knowing what was going to happen to him. It was a nightmare. In the short space of time I had gone from hero to villain.

In true Mickey Thomas style I still made a joke of it once the original shock of being arrested had subsided somewhat. After being released from police custody on bail I went straight around to my best mate Joey Jones' house to meet him and Brian Fian, the manager. I shook hands with Brian and left a tenner in his palm just to break the ice! We all started laughing. It was a real one. Not one of those forged jobs that had got me in lumber. But deep down I still felt gutted that I had been named as part of the scam.

The biggest problem was that one of my bail conditions insisted that I couldn't train at Wrexham for a while as the court had placed temporary ban. I also had to report to the police station at certain times. The whole thing was an absolute nightmare.

So all of a sudden I was back to training on the beach at Colwyn Bay. What would I have done without that stretch of sand near my home? It was the footballing equivalent of being in solitary confinement and absolutely ridiculous. The only time I met my manager and team-mates was for games. Anyway, I had no option but to get on with it.

You can imagine that matches were quite interesting now that the world and its mother knew that I had been arrested over dodgy £10 notes. Not for the first time in my life I was open to abuse and ridicule from the terraces. Opposition fans – those who could afford it – would wave £10 notes at me. When we played West Ham, the Hammers fans, not exactly known for their charity to opposition players, had a field day. We ended up losing but still made a packet for the club – real money, I might add.

But beneath all the black humour was the hurt of having to get on with things for what seemed like an eternity. My mother was ill with cancer and I still had my two kids to look after. In addition, there were countless meetings with the lawyers. Worse still, there were suggestions that if I was found guilty I could expect to go to prison for a couple of years.

What really concerned me was the deteriorating

condition of my mum. She was going in and out of hospital and at times was really ill. She really didn't need me in the midst of a serious court case while she was fighting for her life.

There were a lot of demands on me and to be honest it was all becoming a real bloody pain.

The trial shouldn't have taken eighteen months to come to court but the first hearing was aborted through a legal technicality and so it stretched out to an absurd length of time. I just had to keep going, although it was difficult to concentrate on football. I knew my family needed me. I had no other option.

I know that some people expected me to do a runner. Not at that age, I was too slow! Somehow I got to the end of the season and was thankful that my contract still had another year to run. I heard whispers that some club officials at Wrexham weren't happy with the situation and the adverse publicity I was attracting. Obviously, the fact that I had helped keep Wrexham in business with the goal against Arsenal had been quickly forgotten.

Surely they couldn't have sacked me – you're innocent until proven guilty, aren't you? But football seems to have its own rules so, yes, I was grateful to have another year of my contract to run. In any case, I thought, in the circumstances I had been conducting myself OK. My mother wasn't getting any better so that situation placed everything else in chilling perspective.

It was a hard time for all the family, but as the

breadwinner I knew I couldn't afford to crack. My dad was long gone – and how I wished he had been around. All this was a terrible strain. What was worse was I didn't think I deserved what was happening to me. That win against Arsenal seemed an age ago . . .

Still the wisecracking went on. Everywhere I went people would wave £10 notes in my face. It really got to me, even though I would inevitably smile. In fact, I would have to check before I went into shops to make certain that all my money was real.

What was definitely real was the horrible, gut-churning scenario I found myself in.

Eighteen

By the summer of 1992 I was preparing for my last ever season in professional football. One campaign to go. Christ, where had all the years gone? Suddenly I was facing retirement and a court battle, and all that legal stuff weighed heavily on my mind. Cops, charges, court. Conviction? I couldn't get it out of my head.

I wanted to forget all about that lawyer crap and concentrate on my football. Impossible. I needed a distraction and found it in the warm, welcoming arms of my lover. Sounds perfect, doesn't it? But this is Mickey Thomas we're talking about and when it came to relationships back then – as now – I always landed myself in trouble.

What I didn't figure on was just how much shit I was to find myself in. I had no idea that my latest affair would end in such an explosive climax, so to speak. I can laugh about it now, but I almost didn't survive to tell all the tales in this autobiography. *I was almost bloody murdered.*

Looking back, I was asking for trouble having a fling with a girl called Erica Dean: my sister-in-law, married to my ex-wife's brother. That complication didn't enter my little head when I picked her up in my Volkswagen and stopped in a secluded lane outside St Asaph, in North Wales.

It was the night before the start of the new season and, with hindsight, I should have been suspicious driving to the secluded shagging spot. Glancing into my rear-view mirror, I had spotted a couple of cars following me, their headlights beaming in the dark. I thought, no I couldn't be followed. I just carried on driving, eventually parked up – and got down to business.

We had just started having fun when the nightmare began with a crash of breaking glass. The side window was smashed in and I didn't know what the hell was happening. Don't forget it was pitch black outside and if someone was out to get me I'd been well and truly caught with my pants down, around my ankles to be precise.

I had no idea who the fuck it was. I was giving her one and the next thing coitus is definitely interruptus. I remember wisecracking as the silence became eerie after the windows caved in and glass littered me, the bird and the seats. 'Gentlemen,' I half laughed, 'please let me finish.'

She had said she was kinky, but inviting two guys armed with screwdrivers and hammers was taking her perversion too far. Obviously she knew what was happening. She'd set me up. I'd fallen for the ultimate honey trap.

They came at me from both windows while I was still on top of her in the passenger seat. I was stabbed in the arse with something. I didn't know what it was but I learned later that it was the screwdriver. She wriggled free and did a runner. They then tried to batter me. One of them said, 'We're going to fucking kill you.' They stabbed me again and hit me with a hammer.

That's when I recognised them both. One was her husband. Thank God for that, I thought in another lunatic moment. I was shitting myself in case it was some kind of psychopath.

I was stabbed in my arse, legs, stomach and arm. It was a bloody cowardly attack and I was left bleeding all over. But I kept conscious. I didn't black out and I managed to get out of the car, not really feeling the blows or the pain. That came later. I guess I was in shock. But I came to my senses enough to realise I didn't have the car keys. My attackers had already run off and I was badly beaten up and in the middle of nowhere. I staggered around and managed to flag down a passing car from God knows where.

I must have looked a terrifying sight to the couple in the car, with blood pouring from my battered body. I couldn't have blamed them for driving off instead of picking up this stranger in the middle of the night. But they didn't. They got me in the car and I pleaded with them not to take me to hospital. I got them to drive me home.

When I got through the door, though, and turned on the lights, I realised that I was in a bloody mess. I tried to clean myself up but the wounds were deep and wide. I was in a bad way and I had to get to the hospital. And quick.

I phoned a mate and he took me straight to the Accident and Emergency department, where no sooner had I been admitted and lifted onto a trolley than the police arrived. They wanted me to make a statement and I told them exactly who had attacked me.

The cops immediately issued a search warrant and eventually my attackers were found guilty and jailed for two years. They should have got longer, the bastards.

Anyway, I was patched up and stitched and headed back home in the early hours. It was 6 a.m. and I phoned Joey. Who else? I told him: 'Joey, I can't play today. I've been stabbed.' Over the years I'd made up some good excuses to get out of playing but this was the best. And it was the truth.

I explained to Joey that I had been attacked by two men with a screwdriver and a hammer. 'I know who did it,' he said straightaway. 'They were joiners . . .'. I laughed but I didn't sleep. I was going to go down for forgery. I had been stabbed in the arse. So you could say I was having the time of my life. Having a great time. But even though the pain had now kicked in, I wasn't going to let anyone win. I wouldn't give in and let those two bastards find out I was suffering.

I refused to rest in bed. I couldn't sit down – the pain was too great – so hyper me kept on walking around the house. That didn't help much and it seemed an eternity until the hands on my bedroom clock ticked around to Monday morning.

I went to see the Wrexham physio Steve Wade and he couldn't believe what a mess I was in. He tidied up the wounds, sorted out the butterfly stitches. And the training-ground jokes soon began.

I had ended up with seven arseholes. When I went to jail I was the most sought-after prisoner, I would joke later. With anyone else that vicious attack could have had a shocking effect on the victim. But you know me. I didn't feel like damaged goods. I was back in the news, though, for reasons beyond my control.

It knocked my confidence, particularly when it came to shagging. From then on I made sure all the doors and windows were locked. And after all those blows with screwdrivers and hammers I made sure the tool box was safely locked in the boot.

The horror of it all, to be serious for a moment, made me much stronger, personally, if that was possible. No bastard was going to get me down. I took it on the chin

– and in the arse, obviously. I still had my football to play. The countdown to the end had begun in earnest.

My first game back was against Shrewsbury and I played bloody well. Here I was, back in a Wrexham shirt with holes in my arse playing against a team from Gay Meadow. The irony.

The Wrexham fans were great and happy to see me back in the team after my brush with death. But that last bit of my final season didn't pan out as I thought it would. My last professional game was in the FA Cup against Crewe at Gresty Road on 14 November 1992.

It was the first round proper, but it didn't turn out to be a proper ending for me. In fact, it was a disastrous send-off: we lost 6–1 and I got my marching orders. It was my own fault, although after going 2–0 down by half-time I still hadn't committed a bad tackle. All that was to change after the break.

Crewe scored a third goal at the start of the second half and I heard a shout from a group of celebrating Crewe players. 'Hey, you're going out of the cup, you old git,' said one solitary voice.

For the first time in my life I was looked on as being past it. I didn't know who had said it, but I made up my mind that if I was going out of the cup I was taking one of them with me. I went over the top and the referee's red card ended my involvement with football on sixty minutes. The final hour had tolled.

The referee had been right on the spot and called me to him. 'Five,' he said, pointing to the number on my shirt, 'come over here. That was late.'

I replied with the usual quip: 'I got there as soon as I could, ref.'

He then uttered the last words I would ever hear on a football pitch in a professional game: 'I'm sending you off Mickey, what's your name . . . ?'

He knew damn well. I had made a name for myself in the game and now it was the end of the road. Back in the dressing room, I felt a broken man for the first time in my life. I sat there, head down, thinking seriously about my future. I didn't bloody have one. Maybe, maybe, it was time to pack in. The doubts about carrying on lingered and as I left the ground my mind was in a dark place. Old Father Time had caught up with me and I was in despair.

Sure, Flynnie, Joey and Kevin Reeves tried to keep my spirits up, keep me involved in training. Brian never once called me into his office and told me that it was over. I knew myself. No one had to say anything. But it's strange: the truth that my playing days were over wasn't that hard to stomach. I accepted the end without a fight.

I was thirty-eight and as sad as hell, of course. I was disappointed that everything had come to this.

The end. Not with a bang but a whimper. There was nothing else to do but face the fact that I'd never hear the roar of the crowd again. Never be enveloped by the adulation and warmth of so many fans. Never be the centre of attention in a stadium of 60,000 people.

I was heading for a cell for two in Walton Jail, Liverpool. Wrexham's number five was about to become known as prisoner FGO858 Thomas.

But before that final humiliation came the months of hell, waiting for my fate to be sealed by that bloody judge in Warrington. Court cases came thick and fast and this is where I got so annoyed. At Knutsford Crown Court in Cheshire I arrived believing I would get convicted, only to be met by my co-accused who said, 'I see you are pleading guilty.'

Pleading guilty? No way. Minutes later I went to the court for a meeting with my barrister and my solicitor. I said to them both, 'I have just heard a rumour that you want me to lodge a guilty plea.'

'Yes. Plead guilty,' my barrister said, 'and you won't go to jail.'

This is where I lost it. I went ballistic: 'Hey, I'm not pleading guilty. If I go to jail then so be it. But I'm not pleading guilty to something I haven't done. Get out the room, you're sacked. You've been telling me for eighteen months to plead not guilty.'

My brief left the room but came back ten minutes later and told me he'd be willing to represent me on a not guilty plea. Anyhow, after two days at Knutsford crown court the proceedings were stopped on a technicality. To this day I'm not sure why.

The months of delay were disgraceful. The wait was like seeing the blade of the guillotine glinting in the sun ready to fall and chop off my head. I knew what was going to happen. Because of my reputation the authorities wanted me to go to jail. It was who I was: Mickey Thomas, maverick footballer. They weren't bothered about me as an individual or me as a human being. They just saw Mickey Thomas. He's a name. High profile. Let's get him in jail. But I'd never been in trouble before in my life. That hurt me. I tried to hide my feelings from my kids, Aaron and Jade, and my sick mum, Maureen. I tried to explain gently, to tell them quietly that I might be going away for a little bit. Mum wasn't strong enough to handle the upset. I kept her away from the court appearances. Seeing her little son in the dock would have been too much heartbreak for her.

I didn't let her go to the final court case in Warrington in the July when I was sent down. I still didn't know what to expect but I was told whatever sentence Judge Gareth Edwards declared I could halve it. So eighteen months became nine. And despite being horrified at getting that, I still felt in a strange way a sense of relief. My thoughts were with my mum and kids, though. How would they take the news?

I took comfort that the agonising wait was over as I was led down to the cells below. I had had a noose around my neck for eighteen long months. The trap door had been creaking below me for a long time and now it had sprung open.

But as I endured the long journey to Walton Jail, I obviously couldn't help thinking about my family: how my kids would be affected now Daddy was branded a convict. I was just glad I had the family network to take care of them while I was away. My brother Kevin and sister Pauline were brilliant. My ex-wife Debbie came over as well to help with the kids. She was supportive.

Joey was amazing, too. I needed someone like him to cheer me up as the dark clouds of despair descended. He stuck by me then and always, as now. We're like daft brothers and he promised to visit me in the clink.

I was herded in with some nutters, real hardened criminals, but at the end of the day I knew I wasn't that bad a bloke. I was more Jack the Lad than Jack the Ripper. And as I began the first hour of my sentence I thought back to the start of that crazy day. How my brother Phillip had driven me off after saying my goodbyes. There were no tears from me as I hugged my mum and the kids. I had to be strong.

And you know me, I cracked jokes about Joey bringing me a cake with a file. No one laughed. And then, suited and booted, with a toothbrush in my bag, I climbed into Phillip's car and slowly we left behind my home and family.

I always looked back through the window leaving Colwyn Bay. I still do to this day. But this time the act felt more poignant. I took in the beautiful view, those wonderful mountains. I thought I wouldn't be seeing that panorama for a while. I felt devastated.

I was to be stripped of my dignity in the day that followed but no one could take away my memories. The faces of my gorgeous children could be conjured up in my mind's eye. And replaying my games and goals in my head helped get me through those really horrible first few days in jail. I made up my mind then that I would get the most out of this major crisis in my life. It did help being who I was. A professional footballer. And a person I hoped my fellow inmates would like. Fortunately they did. Well, the majority anyway. They guided me through that alien life on the inside.

I was often in a little world of my own. Even in the darkest moments I could access my brain and remember all those good times on the outside. Many marvellous memories, especially wearing the red shirt of Wales, bellowing out my national anthem before revelling in so many, many glorious nights playing for my beloved country.

Nineteen

From my schooldays, when I couldn't even afford proper football boots, I had always dreamed about playing for Wales.

Once I had proved myself with Wrexham, thankfully, international recognition was to follow. I knew that Mike Smith, the Wales manager at the time, had been keeping a close eye on me. I had also played for Wales at youth level and for the Under 21s and so I was hopeful of making the big step up onto the senior international stage.

To my great delight the opportunity was presented to me when I was called up to face the reigning World Champions, Germany at Cardiff. It was not exactly the easiest of introductions but it was one that I was determined to grab. So there I was, little Mickey Thomas from a Colwyn Bay council estate, reporting for training and I was really nervous being in the company of seasoned Wales stars like Terry Yorath, Dai Davies and Leighton James.

To my eyes it felt like Leighton didn't exactly put me at ease during my first training session. I was practising free kicks when he came over and said to let him take one. It was as if to say, leave it to the real guys, sonny.

But that was quickly forgotten as I was named in the team to face the Germans, and their side was packed with big names, including Franz Beckenbauer, Sepp Maier and Karl-Heinz Rummenigge.

Leighton James was soon at it again. I don't know whether he was trying to put me at ease or it was typical Leighton arrogance, but before the game he told me not to worry about Berti Vogts, who was probably the best full back in the world at the time, because Vogts would obviously be detailed to look after him. Actually, they took Leighton off during that game!

And just to make sure that there was no chance of me getting above my station, John Toshak came out with a cracking remark. Toshack was injured but he was hovering in the dressing room. I was due to wear the number ten shirt and he whispered in my ear not to get too used to that particular shirt because it was his! That wasn't exactly the thing a nervous player wants to hear before the biggest game of his life.

Anyway, as soon as I got on the pitch the nerves disappeared and I was quickly into the swing of things. I destroyed Berti Vogts, who was supposed to be marking me after all and not Leighton. We ended up losing 2–0 but I had made tremendous strides in my career in those ninety minutes. I earned rave reviews and it sparked Manchester United's interest in me. Their manager Dave Sexton was at the game and he was later to sign me.

I suppose when you're young and out on the pitch nothing really inhibits you, and I just felt I was made for international football. I wanted to test myself against the best players in the world and after this experience I couldn't wait for the next Wales game. Later, while we were all in the bath in the dressing room, Terry Yorath told me that I was a good little player. With me playing for Wrexham he probably hadn't seen too much of me and maybe wondered why I was in the team. His comments meant a lot to me.

But there was one big problem for me when it came to international football – my fear of flying. As you know, I've always been petrified of stepping onto a plane. In fact I reckon that this probably cost me another fifty Wales caps. I played for my country fifty-one times – and must have ducked out almost as many times again. It would be the same old scenario time after time: Thomas picked for away game, Thomas goes missing just as the plane is ready to take off. I just couldn't help it, and only those who share the same phobia will understand what I used to go through.

Sometimes I would have driven almost to the airport only to suddenly get the shivers and have to turn the car around and race back home. At first, I would make up an excuse and say that I had been taken ill, but it was obvious to everyone what was happening. I did manage to get on the plane a few times with Wales but only because the team doctor would give me some calming tablets. Even then I was always asking for more – and they didn't really help. It was just an impossible situation.

Mind, all this wasn't helped by a nightmare flight when I was with Manchester United. We were flying down to Gatwick for a game against Crystal Palace and the plane ended up missing the runway. We were being knocked about all over the place and the final straw was seeing one of the air hostesses being sick.

We survived, but you can imagine what that did for what was left of my nerves. It just about finished me off as far as flying was concerned.

I still enjoyed some great games for Wales, although the luck that you need in certain situations never went for us. I truly believe that is one of the reasons why my country have not reached the finals of a major championship since 1958.

Two vital games against Scotland prove my point. You've all heard of Diego Maradona's 'hand of god' goal against England. Well, what about the hand of that sod Joe Jordan against Wales at Anfield in 1977 shortly after I had broken into the side? We knew we had to beat Scotland to have any chance of qualifying for the next year's World Cup finals.

It was a home game but it was being played at Anfield,

home of Liverpool. I remember arriving at the ground in the team coach. All you could see everywhere were Scottish fans. They completely outnumbered the Welsh supporters. Some of them even managed to clamber onto our coach. They were decent and just wanted a bit of fun, but it was still inhibiting.

It wasn't any different inside the ground. There were jocks everywhere. We also knew we were facing a good Scottish side, containing outstanding talent like Kenny Dalglish, Graeme Souness and bloody Jordan. José Mourinho still goes on about the 'ghost' goal against Chelsea, which knocked his side out of the Champions League against Liverpool in 2007. Well, we can still remember the Jordan handball of thirty years earlier!

A ball was swung into the Wales box and a hand – Joe Jordan's hand – could clearly be seen stuck up in the air and making contact with the ball. To our horror, Scotland were awarded a penalty – the referee obviously believed it was a Wales hand that had offended. Don Masson scored with the spot-kick and although Dalglish later scored a second it was the penalty that proved the killer.

I've met Joe many times since – and we were even team-mates for a while at Manchester United – but he still refuses to own up to his crime. It proved a costly one for Wales.

But I suppose football can always be placed in sharp perspective, as was proved when we again met Scotland in another crucial World Cup qualifier, this time at Cardiff's Ninian Park in 1985. Again we needed a win to have any chance of being in the next summer's finals. We led 1–0 until Scotland were awarded another dodgy penalty late on, one that Davie Cooper converted and we again missed out.

But all the Welsh disappointment and Scottish celebrations disappeared when it was revealed that the Scotland manager, Jock Stein, had died of a heart attack immediately after the game. In fact, I still have images in my brain of the medics trying frantically to keep Jock alive as he lay on a bench in the visitors' dressing room. What had preceded this was now completely irrelevant. A great man of football was dead. Nothing else mattered.

The only small consolation for me was that I managed to get Rod Stewart's autograph and later met him with my big mate from The Alarm, Mike Peters. I've got to know Rod over the years and have played in some charity matches with him. He is a great football fan.

There were some magic moments, too, in a Welsh shirt, none more so than a thumping 4–1 win over England at Wrexham. It can hardly get better than that for a patriotic Welshman. England had a fair team at the time, players like Ray Clemence, Ray Wilkins, Peter Barnes, Kenny Sansom. We had a young Ian Rush on the bench. I scored one of the goals and celebrated well into the night. I wasn't the only one: I bumped into the Wales manager Mike England who could see I was well pissed.

There's no problem, he said, because he was actually more pissed than me!

We beat England again in May 1984 at Wrexham, 1–0. It's a pity the Home International championship is no more. It certainly raised the temperature, with countries like ours desperate to beat the old enemy, England. I suppose now, with all the extra commitments in football, it is never going to be resurrected, which is a great pity.

Great victories like these didn't stop me putting the boot into the Welsh FA from time to time. Everything was done on the cheap. We didn't even have decent training gear. We would all have different socks and stuff like that, which is ridiculous for an international side. 'Raggy-Arsed Rovers' we used to call ourselves. We would stay at the cheapest hotels – some of them were an embarrassment – but still you were playing for your country.

I couldn't help making the odd comment, though, to the papers and would receive the inevitable fine. But to be honest, I would have paid for the pleasure of playing for Wales. If only all their games had been at home and not a plane flight away!

Twenty

When you consider some of the great names who have played for Wales, it's a crying shame that the country has not had any real success. We've definitely had great players, great teams – but I'm afraid we've had plenty of bad luck too.

I don't care what anyone says, even those sides who have scaled the greatest heights still need some luck along the way. We seemed forever jinxed when it really mattered – just think of those matches against Scotland, for instance.

But no matter what, no one can argue that over the years I've been involved with my country, Wales haven't had some of the top players. Many of the names I am going to mention now would have been welcomed into any world XIs.

Look at Neville Southall. He might have been a bit of a madcap – after all, he did start life as a binman – but Nev was the best goalkeeper in the world at one time.

There was no arguing about that fact. Rest assured, he would have enjoyed an even bigger reputation if he had played for England. You could make the same statement about Ryan Giggs as well.

Neville had so much confidence about him. He didn't look like a footballer. Sometimes he looked more like a tramp, but no one would dare to tell him that to his face! He was a tremendous performer and was carrying on the tradition of Dai Davies, who was also a top-notch keeper in his day.

Neville was a perfectionist and would train at every opportunity. I remember one day looking out of my hotel window and there was big Nev diving near some flowerbeds on the lawn just below my room. He obviously felt that he hadn't done enough in the team training session earlier in the day. Having Neville behind you was a great start for any team and his confidence helped the mood of the whole dressing room.

And just in front of Nev was his Everton team-mate Kevin Ratcliffe, who also skippered his country later on in his career. He was emerging during my days but quickly matured to become one of the best defenders in the world.

We knew that Gary Speed, another superb player who was going to make his international mark in future years, was once Kevin's paper-boy when they both lived in Hawarden, a village in North Wales. We would say to

Gary that we knew he wouldn't have got any Christmas tips from the Ratcliffe household.

One of Wales' great servants was Terry Yorath and to see what has happened to Terry recently has really hurt. As a player, he was the sort you wanted on your side, certainly not someone to mess around with. He played hard and, yes, at times he could step across the disciplinary line. Without mincing words, he was a dirty bugger.

For Wales he was a vital ingredient in the side. He went on to manage his country and was popular with the players. I remember Yorath's Wales had a chance of reaching the World Cup finals in 1994. They needed to beat Romania in Cardiff in their final qualifying game. I was in jail at the time amongst a group of lifers and so you could say I had other things on my mind. England were also playing that night and so there was no way I was going to contemplate trying to change channels amongst that lot. But the Wales scores were flashed up and they ended up losing, with Paul Bodin crashing a penalty against the bar. What is it with the Welsh and flaming penalties?

It was an awful night all round, with a Wales supporter being killed by a flare that had been launched from the other side of the ground. Sadly, Terry also discovered tragedy at first hand with his fifteen-year-old son dying suddenly while kicking a ball about in the garden.

At the time, Terry put on a brave face and tried to get

on with his life, but the tragedy appears to have caught up with him. He narrowly avoided a prison sentence for killing someone while driving a car but he has struggled to keep his life in check. It's hard to believe, thinking back to that tough guy in the dressing room, but once again football is placed into sharp perspective. It's how you can handle things. At times, as I know, you can't.

Mark Hughes was another combative figure, but he also had fantastic goalscoring skills. I remember him first of all as a shy lad who had been brought up in Ruabon, a village just outside Wrexham. He had started as a midfield player but at Manchester United quickly developed into a prolific striker. I was pretty certain that my fifty-first game for Wales against Hungary was going to be my last – as it proved. Anyway with that knowledge there was only one shirt I wanted after that game and it was Mark's. It might have taken him a little bit by surprise when I made the request because he was still a very humble character. But that showed what I thought of him as a player.

So shy and retiring off the pitch but what a transformation once he was on it. And he became a werewolf or the Incredible Hulk after he had a drink! It was an absolutely amazing character change. But couldn't he score some incredible goals? And if he had listened to me he might now not be credited with that fantastic vollied goal for Wales against Spain at Wrexham, which is often shown on the telly. I remember the cross coming over and me shouting to Mark to leave it to me. Luckily, he ignored my request.

Not only is he one of the best strikers I have ever known he is also one of the best team players. He would put himself about for the good of the team. He was so physically strong. His thighs, for instance, were bigger than my waist. Mark would just get on with the job. He was never one to seek the limelight. He kept himself to himself but, my God, you would have him in your side. Maybe wanting to remain in the shadows as far as his personal life was concerned rebounded on him when he left Manchester United for Barcelona. It didn't work out for him and he quickly returned to Old Trafford, following a spell on loan to Bayern Munich.

He was a wonderful player and I have no hesitation in naming him in the top five players I have known during my career. He's not doing too badly as a manager either. I am not surprised at that because, although he has never been outgoing, he is someone who commands your respect immediately. Fellow professionals want to play for him and that's a great start for a manager.

It was a tough start for any new manager being asked to take charge of Wales but he was the saviour of Welsh football, at the time, after things had gone sour under Bobby Gould. Mark gave the Wales players new belief and a real sense of purpose. The fans flocked back and there were crowds of 75,000 again watching the international side in Cardiff. He had a calmness about him but at the same time an aura.

He did it his way and it was largely successful, even though once again there was nothing at the end of it, with Wales narrowly failing to qualify for the major finals. Even so, he had to put up with some sniping from the likes of John Toshack, who has since discovered to his cost that being in the front is very different to airing your views in a TV studio.

There was no surprise when Blackburn came in for Mark. He has also surrounded himself with a good coaching team, which includes another two Welshmen, Mark Bowen and Eddie Niedzwiecki. I honestly feel that Mark would be the ideal successor to Sir Alex Ferguson at Manchester United once Sir Alex decided to call it a day, even though he's now boss at rivals City. He even has Sir Alex's touchline mannerisms. It would be as smooth a transition as you could possibly get for Mark to move into the Old Trafford hot seat. I believe that the United job wouldn't faze him and deep down I know he would love the job. He has had the right grooming for it in my view.

I don't think many people would argue that they don't come much better than Mark Hughes and Ian Rush when it comes down to striking pairs. That's the combination Wales enjoyed for a number of years. In my view, Rushie is the best goalscorer ever.

Again, like Mark and myself, he came from humble

beginnings, being brought up in the small North Wales town of Rubon. At first, he was naturally very nervous but quickly developed into a fearsome striker – one of the best in the world. I feel a bit guilty now that maybe I took advantage of his nerves when he first came onto the international scene. I would go outside the hotel and ring reception asking for Rushie. When he came to the phone I would pretend to be a reporter and ask him all sorts of stupid questions. Mind, some of his answers weren't that clever either!

But there was nothing wrong with him when he was bearing down on goal. I remember seeing him playing for Liverpool at Aston Villa the night before he was due to report with Wales for the first time and thinking what a striker he was developing into. He just looked a natural goalscorer – and so it proved.

But despite developing into a superstar he has never forgotten his roots and has looked after his family. To me he is a legend but someone who has the common touch. He used to score goals for fun. He even managed to nab one of mine once. We were both in the crowded penalty area waiting for the ball to be delivered. I got the final touch but Rushie was credited with the goal. As if he ever needed any help. Now he is a fantastic ambassador for Welsh football. He is involved in the coaching side of it and would make a good future Wales manager. I'm sure it would be a popular appointment.

Certainly Rushie would be a better bet than John

Toshack in my view. I've already revealed that I wasn't exactly pleased with him when, as a young player, I was warned by him not to get used to the number-ten Wales shirt because it was his. And in the years that have since passed Tosh has never been afraid to voice his opinion. He knows all the answers in front of the TV cameras. It's a pity that is not the case when it comes to being in charge of his national team. There is plenty of work to be done to get back to the level that Mark Hughes attained.

In fairness, Toshack has done well at domestic level. His work with Swansea was phenomenal and he even went on to manage Real Madrid, of course. But for me he has always been someone who believes his opinion is worth more than anybody else's.

I would place him in the same category as another Wales player who didn't lack confidence, Leighton James. He was a good player but always felt he was the star of the side and wasn't slow in reminding you of that. The rest of the lads just used to take the piss out of him behind his back.

We would repeat his story of how his dad told him when he was young that he was going to grow up to be a great player and how he had proved his father right. But it takes all sorts to make up a dressing room. Thankfully, not everyone is like Leighton and Tosh!

Now John Hartson was a different character altogether. I always had a soft spot for John because his dad had been a big supporter of me when I was playing. He would always encourage me and so I would try and look out for John as he was developing into a very good striker. John played a big part in Mark Hughes' Wales side. He wasn't always the fittest but he was a hell of a target man. He was never short of offers from clubs and did particularly well at Arsenal and Celtic.

The one disappointment for John was that he never managed to realise his ambition, which was to play for his home-town club Swansea. He told me once that he had plans to buy it, so you never know what might happen in the future. Maybe he told me because he hoped I might print off some money for him! He has lived a bit and at one time was an addicted gambler. Thankfully, he conquered the habit but he has never been slow to help others who have fallen into trouble. He is forever warning young players about the pitfalls of gambling. He is someone who I believe has a lot to offer, given a chance.

And what about Robbie Savage? What you see is what you get with Robbie. Everyone in football has an opinion about him; he attracts loads of stick. Playing against him, though, is an absolute nightmare and anyone like that is worth their weight in gold in your side. Mark Hughes doesn't suffer fools and he played Robbie all the time for Wales. He also bought him for Blackburn and that says it all for me.

Robbie and I might be chalk and cheese as players but I believe there is room for us both in any side. Robbie is the sort of guy you would have in the trenches with you. Again, he is someone who hasn't forgotten where he comes from. He once told me that he was behind the goal when I scored against Arsenal in the FA Cup. He is a huge Wrexham fan and has said that he wants to play for them before he hangs up his boots. Wrexham might be a better bet than Derby County the way things are going!

He is a great lad, someone who would give you anything. I know he loves the flash things but underneath it all he is an ordinary bloke and a really generous guy.

Gary Speed is another good-guy Welshman and fully deserves the record of having played the most Premier League games. I first saw a young Gary when I was at Leeds. He was coming through the ranks and would end up playing in the title-winning side. One of the things that stood out for me was his heading ability. For a midfield player he was unbelieveable in the air.

Gary has helped me many times in the past. When I was starting out working for Manchester United's football TV station, MUTV, he would always give me an interview. When he was at Newcastle I interviewed him and afterwards he invited me back to his house. He went into the garage and came back with loads of training gear for me. He is a great lad. Last season, when he was at Bolton, he sorted out a couple of tickets for myself and a mate for a game. When we got there he said he wouldn't be doing that again because he had been dropped.

Although he was trying to make a joke about it, I could see he was really hurt and it was no surprise when he soon left to join Sheffield United. But he is a super professional and another possible future Wales manager.

I've been lucky to have known some terrific Wales players. I still think of poor Robbie James who is no longer with us. He sometimes had the misfortune to be my room-mate for Wales games. After one game in Scandinavia I ended up with a local female and didn't get back to the team hotel until just before the team coach was due to leave for the airport. I was panicking. Was I going to make it? I got back to the room in a right old flap to find that Robbie had packed my bag for me. Room-mates don't come much better than that.

Wales have had some top players. They might not have won anything but other countries would often look on with envy at the talent we possessed.

Twenty-one

There was no chance of resurrecting my league career after serving my prison term because time waits for no man, especially when it comes to football. After all the big 40 was rapidly approaching, but that didn't mean I was going to give up playing the game I love. No way.

Thankfully, the phone started ringing with offers and although Inter Cardiff weren't exactly Inter Milan it felt like it to me when they approached me to play for them. They were no mugs, a more than decent League of Wales team who had qualified for that season's European Cup Winners' Cup. That was the tournament that had given me some of the best moments of my career years before with Wrexham.

OUT OF PRISON AND INTO EUROPE screamed the headlines. Mickey Thomas was back on the sports pages once again instead of the front pages. That would do for starters. Here I was at the age of thirty-nine still playing European football. To be honest, I would have settled for playing at any level just to get back. Football is my drug and I simply wanted more.

I had started at the bottom and I might have been going back in that direction but I couldn't have been happier. I knew that some players would be lining up to have a kick at me because of my reputation but I was prepared for that.

It was probably a bit of a publicity stunt for Inter Cardiff as part of their European adventure, but I didn't care. They were also doing me a big favour. I just had one game for them before the European ties came up. The first leg against a Polish team – Katowice – was at home, although Inter Cardiff had to use Merthyr Tydfill's ground because their facilities weren't up to scratch.

We lost – and that was it for me. Because of my fear of flying at the time there was no way I was getting on that plane for the return leg in Poland and after that we decided to call it a day. There would be no more games for Inter Cardiff. It might have been a short and sweet stay but it served its purpose. My new team-mates had accepted me straight away because they could see I was still fit and capable of playing at that level. And as far as the opposition was concerned, again I was used to looking after myself so there were no real problems.

Deep down I knew Inter Cardiff had just really signed me for the European games but I didn't mind. At least people knew I was around playing football again.

It wasn't even a phone call but a knock at the door that

FLASH GUY: Here's me on the bonnet of my gleaming TR7, the first sports car I could afford in my early Wrexham days.

WHO'S THAT? Me, of course, pictured by a new pal on one of my many runaway jaunts to Marbella in Spain.

GIVE US A SIGN I'm back at school signing autographs for the kids in their classroom.

GEORGOUS
Boy George isn't
bad either as I get
to know him during
a video shoot at
Stamford Bridge.

MANIC...Meet Nicky Wire,
the wonderfully talented guitarist
with Manic Street Preachers,
who like me is a footie nut.

PREACHER MAN...Here's yours truly
with James Dean Bradfield the fabulous
lead singer with Manic Street Preachers.

THE THREE OF US Myself Jade and Aaron enjoy the good life during my time in America.

MIDDLE MAN I couldn't be in better company than George Best and Rod Stewart during a soccer six competition at Stamford Bridge.

PLEASE RELEASE ME One of my frequent pass outs from Foston with my full name, address and prison number.

ONE FOR THE ROAD I couldn't speed in this monster as I return to my road digging days, pictured with my 'boss' Ricky Fryer.

IVY LEAGUE That's me with TV legend Michael Parkinson at The Ivy in London with my pals Mike Walsh (right) and Sean Walsh.

TAKE THAT Here I am in an all-star studded line-up for a game at Rhyl with Take That's Mark Owen, Tim Lovejoy, Alan Kennedy and John Barnes to name but a few.

MEN UNITED What a team and what an honour, thanks to Manchester United, to be photographed with greats like Norman Whiteside, Paddy Crerard, Paul Parker, Wilf McGuinness, Lee Martin, Rio Ferdinand, Wayne Rooney, Cristiano Ronaldo and Ruud van Nistelrooy.

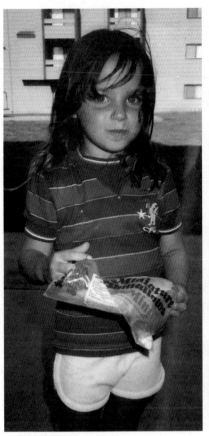

THREE OF A KIND Boxing champ Joe Calzaghe
gives me a playful dig alongside my good friend
from Cardiff Ian Waters.

DADDY'S GIRL Jade tries out her brand new
Chelsea shirt for size in America.

JUST THE TWO OF US Jade and her fresh
faced dad relax away from the rigours of
indoor football in the States.

KIDS STUFF
Here I am taking time out
from playing, again in
America, to be with the kids.

SMILES AWAY
My lovely Jade takes time
on an exhausting car journey
to show the camera just
how beautiful she is.

BOXING CLEVER
My son Aaron has a break from
his punishing training schedule
to put his fists up.

HAPPY FAMILY
My mum's brother Teddy
and her sisters Kathleen
(next to me) and Trudy.

KNOCKOUT
Jade pictured after winning
one of her kick boxing
tournaments.

presented me with my next chance to continue my career – with a rough-and-ready Sunday League side called The Arabs, who were based down the road at Llandudno! They might have enjoyed a few drinks and some scraps but they were really good down-to-earth lads. I even ended up winning a medal with them. I think they were as surprised as me when they knocked on my door asking whether I was interested in turning out for them. I said yes straight away. I don't think they were expecting that.

I ended up playing Bernie Head on five or six games for them and we reached the final of the local Sunday cup, which was staged at Prestatyn Town's ground. Back in the big time, eh! There was even a bit of a fight in that final but that's quite normal at that level.

One of their players came up to me before the game and warned me that he was after me – he was going to kick me until I was black and blue. I asked him where he was from and he replied Flint. I said that he must know my big mate Ian Rush, then, because he's from Flint. Oh, came the reply, if I knew Rushie then he would let me off.

Anyway, we ended up winning the game and there was another medal to add to my collection. We had a big drink afterwards. It's what football is all about. Fantastic.

I was on a roll now and soon another Welsh League side, Porthmadog, came calling. So no more games with The Arabs! I knew the manager, former Crystal Palace striker Ian Edwards, and he asked me to come on board.

I played a few games before they got rid of Edwards and the people who run the club asked me to take over. As I've said before, I could barely manage myself never mind managing a Welsh League side. But I decided to go for it, so suddenly I was Mickey Thomas, player-manager of Porthmadog.

Believe it or not, I actually lasted a season in the job. I was quite easy-going, but the one thing I wouldn't stand for was my players going out on the Friday night and having a few drinks on the eve of the game. Yes, I know, I did it enough times but I wasn't going to let any of my players get away with it. Talk about the poacher turning into a gamekeeper.

I don't think I even missed any of the training sessions I was taking. I suppose at last it gave me an insight into management and what it was all about. I always knew I had been a pain in the arse for many of my managers. This confirmed it, because now I was on the other side. The most difficult thing, having played at a higher level, was having to accept that your players can never get near your own standards. It would have been so easy to have had a go at them but I had to hold back.

There were some decent players but also some nutters, but somehow I managed to keep everything in order. I helped our cause by bringing in a more experienced head in Colin Hawkins, who had a decent reputation on the North Wales coast. He became my assistant and we worked well together. There were many frustrations, the biggest being that we had no money to entice some of the better players to Porthmadog. Eventually, my fire went out and I'd had enough. There was no big fall-out, I just decided to move on. I'd had a go at it but deep down I knew that football management wasn't really for me. I just wanted to play without any worries.

I soon got that wish when Tommy Charlton, who was the manager of Amlych Town, who were based on the island of Anglesey, asked if I was interested in playing for them. He told me I would get £20 a game! OK, it wasn't a fortune and this was a level below the Welsh League, but I went for it as there were some good players in the team, like Merv Williams, the goal keeper, Mark Way, Nigel Ault, the assistant manager, pete O'Neill, Viv Williams and Andy Stewart. I didn't have a car at the time so Tommy would always pick me up. There would only be a man and a dog watching the games but that didn't bother me either. Some of the pitches we played on weren't marked out properly and you would have to dodge the sheep droppings but I was playing the game I love – and without a real care in the world.

There was a great atmosphere surrounding that little club. I would always have a drink with the lads afterwards and they would sit there transfixed as I recounted some of my stories from the past. They couldn't get enough of them and as long as I was chasing a ball again I was like, well, a pig in sheep dung!

Eventually I got tired of the trips because it was a fair

old hike all the time to Amlych and when Pete Parry the chairman of Rhyl asked me to come on board I couldn't turn the offer down. It was just down the road for me and Pete was very ambitious. He asked me to become the club's director of football. First management and now director of football. I was really moving in strange circles now . . .

Pete had his head screwed on. He wanted me to utilise my contacts to attract the Football League clubs to Rhyl for some lucrative friendlies and to help put the League of Wales side on the footballing map. I managed that OK. Andy Ritchie's Oldham came down, Joe Royle, who was boss of Manchester City, brought his side. Some of my former clubs – Derby County, Stoke, Everton – all came to Rhyl. Everyone was obviously delighted with that and I felt good because I knew the club's finances would be healthier through my work.

One of the most satisfying moments of my time at Rhyl was when Pete Parry and I discovered striker Lee Trundle, who was later to command a £1 million transfer fee. He cost Rhyl just £10,000. We had gone to watch Colwyn Bay because we had a player in mind who we wanted to sign. Lee was playing for the opponents and he ended up scoring five goals. I turned around to Pete and said to him, 'If you've got the money, buy him.'

It was a great piece of business because Lee went on to join Wrexham, became a goalscoring hero at Swansea City and moved to Bristol City for £1 million.

He has established himself as a leading striker in the Championship and just missed out on playing in the Premier League, Bristol City losing to Hull in the play-off final at Wembley in May.

It's all about giving raw players their opportunity. There are good players in the lower leagues but not enough bigger clubs are prepared to take a chance. You also need a bit of luck to succeed. I remember phoning Mark Wright, who was then the manager of South Port what he thought of Lee Trundle cos we wanted to sign him at Rhyl. He told me he thought Lee was a bad lad and wasn't worth bothering with. So I put down the phone and told the Rhyl chairman Pete Parry what he said, so he said 'What do you think?' and I said 'people have said bad things about me and I've proved them wrong. Let's take a chance on him.' Luckily for Lee, Wrexham went for it and they got their rewards after making a huge profit when Swansea bought him.

Players at this level need encouragement. They also need managers to get off their backsides and take a look, instead of just going through countless DVDs of foreign players. There is talent out there; it's a case of going out and looking for it.

I enjoyed my time at Rhyl. Now I'm helping out along the road at Prestatyn Town. It's nothing big because my media commitments prevent me from being at most of their games. It's just a case of trying to arrange some celebrity games and doing a few talk-ins. It means I'm still involved in football at that level. Hopefully, this typifies what I'm about. I still want to give something back and, although I'm well into my fifties now, I am fit and able to play the odd charity game or Masters game.

I would like to think I have never forgotten my roots. As a kid I would never stop kicking a ball on a field or on the beach. There's no way I'm stopping now.

Twenty-two

The threats, kicks and whacks from my time in the non-league game made me smile, as I would think back to the many dust-ups in my days playing at the highest level. That was the era of the real hard men. Not like some of the powder-puff merchants parading on our Premiership pitches today, clutching their faces and crashing to the ground when their mascara runs.

Go back even further and remember the likes of Dave Mackay, that legend of Tottenham and Scotland: Leeds' great Johnny Giles; Manchester City's brilliant goalscorer Francis Lee, and the late Billy Bremner. They would have made my hair curl if I'd had any left. They didn't hold back. Men's men. Battle-hardened international players who weren't afraid to stand up for themselves.

I still shudder at some of the X-rated scenes I witnessed both on the training ground and in the dressing room. Those bust-ups rarely became public knowledge. And I must admit that many scraps happened right under my nose and I immediately dismissed them as 'handbags' at dawn.

My mate Joey, though, always took more notice than me and can vividly recall fights between so-called team-mates. That was probably because in our time together at Chelsea he was often the unofficial referee, standing between players to end these impromptu bouts.

Most of the time the Chelsea camp was a happy one, but at times rows would break out in five-a-sides or after games. And one player was always at the centre of the outbreak of war – David Speedie.

Speedie could argue with his own shadow and often wasn't that clever about picking a fight with an opponent. Big defender Paul Canoville or Kerry Dixon were obvious examples of Speedie punching above his weight. Mind you, everyone in the team, except little old me, was bigger and stronger than Speedie.

Not that that stopped him having a right go whenever he lost that infamous temper of his. Speedie always wanted to fight with everyone and anyone. He was so aggressive. It was in his nature. But he did ask for trouble. We all knew that Kerry Dixon was a perfectionist in and out of the dressing room. He would always lay his kit out on the bench in such a precise manner. Talk about neat and tidy. So it wasn't the wisest thing to do to chuck his clothes on the floor when he went for a piss.

But Speedie never held back. Joey remembers stopping a couple of fights between him and big Canoville on the training ground.

One of them was a belter, a real fight. Canoville was built like a middleweight boxer. It was bang, bang, bang. They called him King Canoville and he was a difficult man to stop once the red mist filled his eyes.

Joey said he struggled to hold him in a headlock in that fight with Speedie. He fought hard to hold him back. Canoville made no bones about it: he wanted to kill Speedie, but eventually Joey made him see sense and calmed him down before Speedie was totally flattened and out for the count.

Even then Speedie wasn't safe. Let me tell you, there were a handful of other Chelsea players ready to pile in and have a go at him. He could rub you up that way. Talk about lighting the blue touch paper and standing back ready for the resulting explosion.

I remember playing against Sunderland and I wanted to put the ball into the box for him first time so he could have a go at goal. But the ball bobbled so I couldn't actually make the pass. Well, Speedie stood there waving his arms, furious with me. I told him straight not to wave his fucking arms at me and that was that.

But Speedie was an incident waiting to happen and on another occasion he had a fight in the dressing room with Dixon. They were great on the pitch together. Speedie was a great foil for Dixon and made a lot of goals for him.

But in one game, Dixon could have passed to Speedie but he obviously wanted to shoot himself. He missed and Chelsea lost. In the dressing room, Speedie gave Dixon a right mouthful about not passing the ball to him. Dixon was a hard lad and banged him. Boom. Served him right.

Having said that, Speedie was the type of lad you always wanted in your team. He was a great player, a competitor. He scored a lot of important goals for Chelsea – he just upset a lot of people in the process.

Speedie was volatile with a capital 'V'. Joey said the little man had twelve fights in his career – and never won one. Mind you, we could all lose our heads in that Chelsea side. We all got banned from the players' lounge at Sunderland once because of previous with their players. A few fights here and there on the pitch meant we weren't welcome. That was a bit bizarre, to say the least. If there's any trouble, any bad blood, it should always be forgotten when that final whistle goes.

The biggest bust-up I ever saw came in my impressionable early days at Wrexham. And boy did that scrap open my eyes to the harsh world of professional football. We had a big centre-half and captain in those days, Eddie May. He went on to make 334 appearances for Wrexham but it was in one game at York where he became a knockout in my eyes – literally.

After the final whistle the dressing room became a boxing ring. Eddie had a right go at our goalkeeper, Brian Lloyd, a lovely lad. He was a self-employed design consultant who later in life won awards for his architectural work. Well, let's just say he was well and truly demolished with a couple of Eddie's swinging right and left hooks.

Eddie gave him a real bruising and I just thought, Welcome to the real world of football, Mickey.

Not that I swung that many punches in my career. I've admitted to a few and I can honestly say that I was furious in my short spell at Everton when I was singled out for criticism by a team-mate called Trevor Ross.

We were playing at Stoke. They scored a goal and Ross started pointing the finger at me as if it was my fault. I squared him up at half-time and told him, 'Point that finger at me again and I will snap it off you prick. Don't try and belittle me.'

Even if you know you have probably done wrong out there on the pitch, you don't want a little shit pointing the finger of blame at you.

Arguments, rows and punch-ups are part and parcel of football. I always used to have a go at Tottenham's Steve Perryman. He was an aggressive type of player and I loved our ding-dongs. Graeme Souness was the best, though. He had a skill no other player possessed:

Souey could kick you in the same spot three times in quick succession. That was great precision, great skill. And it bloody hurt. He gave me a few whacks in our battles together and I gave it him back, too. Jimmy Case was another hard lad. I loved him. You knew what was coming from Jimmy. But he would take it as well. He seemed to enjoy the pain.

I used to hate playing against Sammy Nelson and Pat Rice at Arsenal. There was no messing with those two. They didn't have to go very high to take me off at the head. I was never as hard as them but I could always look after myself in a tough world.

Looking back, though, the biggest thumps I got were the ones I appreciated and loved: the heavy pats on the back from Chelsea supporters who I will never forget for immediately taking me to their hearts in my time at Stamford Bridge. I will always remember a great piece of advice from Joey before I made my debut. Joey told me to run to Gate 13 at Stamford Bridge if I ever scored a goal. I did, of course, in that opening home game against Sheffield Wednesday and immediately I was off, heading for that section where the real fans were housed.

I jumped on them beyond Gate 13 and they jumped all over me, hugging and kissing me in a show of real affection, which I like to think has remained to this day. I had a great rapport with the Chelsea supporters. They respected me and, for me, you can't get better than that.

From that precious first moment in their welcoming arms I was dubbed the King of King's Road. Much better than the Queen of Queen's Road . . .

Twenty-three

Now most of you will still have this image of me with that mass of back hair, creating mischief wherever I went. It's in stark contrast to the photograph of me on the front of the book, as bald as a coot.

So where did it all go? Has it been some sort of fashion statement? Did I suddenly wake up one morning and decide on a new look?

There's one simple answer to all that. This happy-go-lucky character was almost destroyed by nerves. Although, in the end, I managed to survive, my hair didn't – and to be honest I'm not bothered.

I first really noticed my hair thinning out as I had that long wait for my court appearance over the forged tenners. In fact, it wasn't just thinning out, it was dropping out rather alarmingly. There was no hiding it, I was losing my hair. For some people it might seem like the end of the world – not for me. My nerves might have been shredded to bits and that was reflected in the hair loss, but I had more important things to worry about.

My mum, who had stood by me throughout the highs and lows, was slowly dying in front of my eyes. The stomach cancer that had brought her world and mine crashing wasn't going to go away.

Everything that could go wrong was going wrong. I had this interminable wait for the case to come to court with the distinct probability that after it I would lose my freedom: my mother was seriously ill and my football career was in its twilight years. So what did it matter that my hair was on the way out?

I suppose many of the football memories are of me skipping down the wings with my long hair flowing in the breeze. Even Jimmy Floyd Hasselbaink said to me a few years ago after we were introduced, 'I know you, long black hair.' Hopefully, there was more to me than that but I knew what he meant.

OK, it was once one of my trademarks but you just have to get on with it. I am certain the damage to my roots was caused by all the anxiety of the impending court case. At first, like many people do, I just left my thinning hair alone, pretending it was the same as it had always been. But then even I started to realise that it looked ridiculous. I know some people had been giving me strange looks about the disappearing hair for some time.

In the end, my daughter Jade, who was only young at the time, told me to shave it off. Those words hit home.

Even she thought I looked stupid. You can't fight the inevitable and so up I went into the bathroom and shaved my head. I felt respectable again, instead of some joke figure pretending he was still a youngster.

To my delight the new look was accepted straight away and in many ways I'm just as recognisable now without any hair as I was with those flowing locks. Anyway, as usual my mate Joey Jones could always see the funny side. He told me if I went to jail with long hair my arse was in danger of becoming a bit sore! Thanks, Joey . . .

But one thing neither of us could see the funny side of was the decline of my mum. What was really eating into me was the fact that I had been on the other side of the Atlantic when my dad died. Now there was a chance that I would be behind bars, unable to be at my mum's side when the end came for her. My mum was so ill that there was talk of my son Aaron going to live with Joey and his wife Janice. This was a really horrible period and it placed a terrible strain on the family.

It was doing my head in, because I felt so guilty placing extra strain on my mum with everything that was happening off the pitch. I used to lie awake at night worrying about what was going to happen to my family.

The one consolation – if you can really call it that – was that I was around when my mum eventually died. She had dragged out her fight against cancer far longer than the medical people had predicted, which was a credit to her courage and fortitude – typical of my mum.

She had been my rock, there to help at every opportunity. She had always been there for me. But knowing there was no hope didn't make it any easier when she passed away. I felt utterly destroyed, helpless, and wondered what lay ahead. I was frightened.

Joey, as usual, was fantastic and did everything he could to help me through the biggest ordeal of my life.

We were so close. For instance, who else would sleep with the best man on the night before his wedding? That's what Joey had done to make sure that I made it to his wedding, and you thought it was all about the best man ensuring that the groom got to the altar in time! You can't blame him: at the time I had such a big reputation for going missing. In addition to making me sleep in his bed with him the night before the big day, he had also put another mate on stand-by in case I still managed to do a runner!

My mum wanted to die in our home – in fact, in the bedroom where I was born. Sadly, that wasn't the case because to try to ease her suffering in those final hours she was moved to a hospice where they could care for her better. She passed away there. It was horrendous. Suddenly the strongest person I had known in my life was no longer there for me.

At least her memory lives on because I have never moved house. I'm still in the same place, which has been my home for all the years that I've been on this earth.

Often people have wondered why I have never moved. It's simple. I was born there, I'm happy there and I've never been one to worry about image. I wouldn't care if it was the roughest place on earth – which it isn't, by the way – it's where I feel more comfortable.

It's where, thanks to my family, I've shared my happiest moments. Still to this day, though, I have guilt feelings about my mum's last few months. Despite being really ill, she still had time to support me as I went through my own dark time. She never thought any less of me, though. She was still proud of me, but that's mums for you, isn't it?

We've had some happy times all of us. I still laugh at one incident involving my dad. At the time he had a bit of a drink problem. He needed some money and so I told him to meet me at Rhyl station where I would be on the train and I would give him what he wanted. He would just have to get on and off the train while I continued my journey, simple.

Well, it didn't turn out that way. After sorting him out I thought that was it and he was on his way. Strangely, the train stayed in the station for what seemed ages. Eventually, the guard came up to me and explained that my dad had caused the delay – obviously the worse for wear for drink, he had exited the train through the wrong door. Instead of stepping onto the platform, he had fallen on to the tracks on the other side of the carriage. Luckily, he had escaped any real damage.

We've had some great times as a family and what you can't do is take away those memories, so there's no way I will be uprooting now. I know I could get something that would be 'better' in many people's eyes, but not in mine and that is what is important. I'm not interested in a more salubrious house. I don't think having a palatial pad makes you a better person. A home is a home, not a pile of bricks.

Here I know I can leave my front door open at night – not that there is anything to pinch – and I've had the same neighbours for years. I've even asked my kids whether they want to move and they have always said no.

Good on them, chips off the old block. There have been conflicting emotions in that house, many of them I have already described to you. But life goes on, hopefully for some time yet.

Twenty-four

My mate Joey has always trodden a well-worn path to my house. And I thank God he did when I first came out of prison. Without being a drama queen, he basically saved my life. I have had a lot of debts in my life but I owe the biggest one to Joey. You need someone to inspire you in life and he was definitely my inspiration. His words of encouragement have been immense.

I pretty much disappeared off the face of the planet in those first few weeks after being released from prison. I always said that, even in my darkest hours, I would never have committed suicide. But I must admit there were times when I felt like slitting my throat.

I might have been Mickey Thomas no more. You get like that when you can't take any more, when life has kicked you so hard in the balls that you sit there thinking, What's the bloody point? Joey always jokes that I phoned the Samaritans once and they put the phone down on me.

I did call them in my darkest moment to say I'd been thinking about suicide. I told this woman my problems and didn't know it was her first night. She said, 'I'm new to all this. I'm going to have to ask my boss what advice I can give you.' She was gone about fifteen minutes and came back to the phone to tell me, 'I have had a word with my manager and he thinks you are doing the right thing.'

Joking apart, I wouldn't be who I am today without Joey. When I came out of the nick, I spoke to him on a regular basis, every other day. Joey made it his mission to get me back on my feet and think up ways of making me some money because I was flat broke. Joey always laughs that he got me the job on Sky – putting up satellite dishes on the sides of houses.

I was really struggling but Joey kept on and on at me about doing some TV work. He said when I got serious and stopped clowning around I could be as good as any football pundit on the box. He kept faith in me. Made me believe in myself again.

I will always remember him coming round to my mum's house when I was in an emotional and financial mess after coming home from prison. I had no food in the house. As I said earlier, I ripped up my mum's sofa to find some loose change to buy a jacket spud. But Joey and his missus Janice brought me a bag of groceries: bread, butter, cheese and meat. God, I was so grateful for that.

It was good to see the two of them again. I hadn't felt like seeing too many people but their smiling faces gave me a real lift. They must have wondered what was going on. There were no curtains up at the windows of our house and I'd daubed the glass with a bottle of cleaner called Windolene. From inside I wrote in big letters: *Fuck off.* That summed up my feelings to the outside world. It was a heartfelt message to anyone and everyone.

Joey just laughed. That tickled him. But I was at rock bottom below the bloody rock. I had nothing to my name. I had a few clothes, nothing decent, and a pair of shoes with big holes in the soles. I ripped up a cardboard box and put pieces inside the shoes to keep out the water.

At Ian Rush's testimonial in 1994, I was so ashamed about being so broke. I changed next to those footballing greats Alan Hansen and Kenny Dalglish and I prayed that after the game they didn't pick up my shoes by mistake. How embarrassing. Here I was in a dressing room with so many millionaires and I had a pair of cardboard shoes walking down skid row.

But back to Joey. He always said I had changed dramatically on my release. And he wasn't just talking about me not wearing a prison uniform or a ball and chain round my ankle. He was so glad to see me a free man after being so devastated when I was sent down. Joey has told me many times since that he wouldn't have been surprised if he had got a call a few weeks into my sentence telling him that I had topped myself in my cell.

He knew what I was like in confined spaces. He knew I couldn't keep still. He was convinced that I would end it all and he told Janice his fears that I wouldn't be able to hack it behind bars. Joey was worried because I always did things on the spur of the moment. He knew from past experiences what I was like. He still reminds me of our time together as apprentices in those Wrexham digs when I nipped out for a bottle of milk and didn't come back for two weeks.

When people ask Joey to describe me he's the first to admit I'm mad – off my head. But I was never quite daft enough to seriously think about committing suicide. I would never have left my kids without a dad – or Joey without a best mate. We have known each other for almost forty years and I know he regards me as a brother. I feel the same.

Joey has got a heart of gold. But that huge ticker of his almost packed in on him when he had to undergo major surgery to repair a dodgy heart valve. I was the first at his bedside along with Janice when he was admitted to hospital after that major heart scare six years ago.

I was there every day with him after picking Janice up from their lovely home in Wrexham. I would drive every day from Colwyn Bay to Wrexham and on to his hospital in Liverpool. I tried to make him laugh but I'm sure I was a pain in the backside with my attempt at humour. When he first came out of the operating theatre I could see he was in real agony. Finally he woke up and the first thing I said was, 'They should have operated on your face, you ugly bastard.'

Anyone who said he was looking well I would chip in with, 'Don't tell him lies. Joey, you look as though you aren't going to make it, mate.'

Joking apart, my poor pal had gone through a major operation, although he always said it was just a routine procedure. Routine? Christ, his operation took four hours. They even took his heart out of his body, yet he says it was nothing. That's typical Joey. It was bloody scary for everyone. The whole of football was stunned because he was such a fit bloke.

The doctors told Joey that he had been born with the problem. Seemingly, he could have dropped down dead at any time, even as a kid. But he played all his wonderful career with it. Amazing. It certainly brings you down to earth when your pal is struck down with heart trouble.

You would never have guessed Joey would suffer from an ailment like that. Mind you, not many people know to this day that I had problems with my heart, too. When I went from Manchester United to Everton they stopped the signing. After exhaustive tests, the specialist at my medical said there was something wrong with my heart .

They sent me to hospital straight away and strapped me up to all kinds of wires and whirring machinery. But as fast as the 'problem' was spotted it disappeared. My mind was in a whirl, thinking my career was over, but I was given the all-clear and the deal went through.

I thought that was the end of it, but later, when I went to Brighton from Everton, another specialist told the club that I had a problem with my heart. He said it was missing a beat but that he'd never seen a heart like it. I remember him saying, 'You must be super-human fit. You have the biggest heart I have ever seen. It's massive.'

The so-called problem didn't bother Brighton, though. They were still prepared to pay the £500,000 transfer fee and carried on with the deal. It wasn't a risk. I never had complications or suffered any pain. It never bothered me or affected my stamina. In fact, it was quite the opposite. I was as strong as an ox. The only problem with my heart was that it kept on getting broken but I'm never the kind of person to dwell on relationship break-ups.

I'm just happy to have had Joey by my side when things went wrong. That's why I was delighted to stand by him when his life was thrown into turmoil the way he's always stood by me. He has always been the voice of sanity when I was lost in the wilderness. And he moved heaven and earth to get me back on my feet.

Joey has been at my side since we were fourteen and starting out on that early footballing road to Wrexham. And all those years later, when I wanted to keep myself to myself as a free yet sad man, Joey was the one to drag me up off my knees. Unknown to me, his dad Harry was a massive help, too. God rest his soul.

Harry wasn't happy that local people had turned their

backs on me because of the stain on my character. And so he wrote a letter to the local paper without telling the editor that he was Joey's dad. He said that I shouldn't be judged by what had gone on with the prison sentence. That I had been a great ambassador for Welsh football. Everyone made mistakes and that what had happened had happened.

The letter was printed and when I found out who the author was I phoned Joey and asked him to thank his dad. Those kind words meant so much. He wanted everyone to know, in case there was any doubt, that Mickey Thomas wasn't a bad lad. And I will always be grateful for that show of faith in me.

Just when you think no one cares, someone like Harry took the time and the trouble to tell all my neighbours in Colwyn Bay that I deserved to be given the chance to bounce back to my old self.

It took a while but I got there . . . with even more help from Joey and another great, great guy: good old Tim Lovejoy.

Twenty-five

My introduction to Tim and my involvement with Sky came totally by chance. I switched on the TV one Saturday morning and Tim was on his famous *Soccer AM* show with the lovely Helen Chamberlain. He was asking former Chelsea great Clive Walker who was the maddest footballer ever. Clive didn't hesitate: Mickey Thomas, he declared. I couldn't believe it, seeing my face on the telly. I felt alive and kicking again.

Talking about me must have triggered a thought in Tim's brain and a couple of weeks later I got a call from the Sky studios inviting me to appear on *Soccer AM* for what turned out to be the first of many, many guest appearances. I was made up.

Tim, of course, was a Chelsea nut and had great admiration for me and other Bridge players he had cheered from the terraces. He had a lot of respect for Joey, too. It was a big boost for me knowing that Tim was on my side. He fronted such an iconic footballing programme, which was, and still is, a major cult show with the fans.

The more appearances I made with Tim the more people welcomed me back into their arms. Over the months, I started to become a bit of a household name once more. So I can thank Tim for kicking off my media career and giving me the chance to start all over again. My confidence and self-belief soared.

Tim was fabulous with me on our first meeting. The warmth of his greeting is something I will never forget. He put me at ease straight away and made me feel so special. He sunk straight to his knees and bowed before me. I could have bloody cried. Tim just said, 'Mickey, you are my hero.'

I'm only a little guy, as you know, but at that moment I felt ten foot tall. Tim has told me since that I am his all-time favourite and he will never forget that cheeky wink on *Match of the Day*. We will always remain friends.

Through his first kind invitation to appear on his show I got my first big cheque since playing football in the big time. The money started to come in, albeit slowly at first. In fact, I did a lot of TV and radio appearances for nothing, just to get myself noticed again.

Tim was brilliant to me. The same can be said for pals like Peter Reid and Graeme Souness, who both encouraged me to get into the media spotlight – to use my name to make a living. I explored every avenue and Joey put the idea into my head that I should join the after-dinner speaking circuit and tell an audience the raw truth of my life.

But don't think for a moment that the bookings flooded in for the likes of the Savoy in London or other palatial settings up and down the country. No. I began very much at the bottom, touring working men's clubs, insisting that all I would entertain were question-and-answer sessions. I wasn't brave enough to stand on my own two feet and address an audience of sport lovers.

And I didn't have enough confidence to go on the circuit alone. Fly solo. Yes, you've guessed it, I begged Joey to come with me. He wasn't that keen. Joey doesn't like public speaking but he wasn't going to let me down.

The only trouble I had was calming my nerves. So I turned to drink to give me some Dutch courage, just as I had on those Friday nights before appearing at Old Trafford, when I had turned to a much-loved wine bottle or two. The problem was that I didn't know when to stop. I downed drinks as fast as I delivered the one-liners. Sometimes I'd supped so much I didn't know where I was or what I was saying.

I hit the bottle hard every night. On one occasion there was a lull in the questions and Joey said I just stood up and told the audience, 'Anyway, I'm an alcoholic.'

Right out of the blue. Joey looked stunned and said, 'Why did you say that?'

I swayed, stared back at Joey and replied, 'I couldn't think of anything else to say.'

We took a wee break and I headed back to the bar. When the second half of the show started, a bloke stood up and said, 'I want to congratulate you for coming out and saying that.'

I got a standing ovation. Perhaps I was an alcoholic then. I don't know. I admit, though, that I drank heavily.

I always got so wound up and worried about doing the shows. It got from bad to worse. From downing a couple of stiff ones before going on the stage, it increased to four, five, six double brandies – maybe eight, I can't remember. I probably downed a whole bottle of the stuff. Many times I was totally wasted.

Those audiences became a blur of fuzzy faces. I can't even remember half the answers I gave to their probing questions. It's strange thinking back, especially now that I don't touch a drop of alcohol. I can address a VIP audience, appear on TV, run through a radio summary, and I don't need a drink to get me through it. Just tea for me, these days – plenty of milk and sugar.

But back then, the hard stuff almost became as big a friend as Joey. I definitely couldn't get enough. Joey always reminds me about one function at Lancaster where I stood with a tumbler full of brandy in my hand and told everyone that I had a drink problem.

With that, I flung the drink straight past my ear and it splashed on the wall behind. 'That's the problem,' I said. 'I can't always find my mouth.'

Joey wasn't amused. I was on another road to ruin but he was determined I wasn't going to end up in a drinking hell. He told me bluntly that the audience had paid good money to hear my stories. If they wanted to hear a rambling piss-head they could do that any night of the week down at their locals.

There were no quips, no jokes. Joey was deadly serious that I had to stop drinking. He was worried about me, and after twelve months of me getting leathered he'd had enough. I felt the same but I still craved the drink to calm the nerves. Then one morning I just woke up and thought, That's it, I've got to stop. And I did.

After that, I could drive to functions for the first time with Joey as my passenger – not slumped in the back seat of his car feeling shit and wanting to throw up all the time. Although on one trip to Shrewsbury he still wouldn't get in the car with me for very different reasons.

We were booked at, of all places, the Shrewsbury police club. Quite ironic, I thought, after the boys in blue had arrested and charged me back in Colwyn Bay. At that time I was still cleaning cars to earn some extra cash and Joey told me to be at his house in Wrexham in plenty of time so he could drive me to the venue. By 6 p.m. I still hadn't arrived and he phoned me panicking. I told him I was on my way.

How could I get there in time? I thought. Easy. I'll just take one of the cars I had been cleaning from the forecourt. So I pulled up at Joey's place in this car with the £1,800 price tag on the widescreen. I just ripped it off and threw it on the back seat before Joey came out.

The 'nicked' car had no tax and I wasn't insured. Every tyre was bald. And I was going to talk to about five hundred coppers. Surprisingly, Joey wouldn't get in with me. He opted to travel in his own car and I followed in the hot wheels behind. I found the police club and pulled up in their car park as bold as brass: a former jailbird in a dodgy car, parked in full view of all those cops.

They gave me a great welcome and loved my tales of prison life, especially in Walton Jail. I must admit they were pretty shocked when I told them how much time I did behind bars. But they would have been even more stunned if they had known I drove home that night in a car without tax or insurance.

Somehow, trouble still followed me around. As you've read, I got into some scrapes throughout my colourful life. And you could always guarantee that my loose tongue would regularly land me in the shit. A slip live on air in one of my first radio jobs almost got me banned from the BBC. I was given the summarising job for an FA Cup tie between Oldham and Swansea. I was doing the scheme with Rob Philips, an experienced guy from the BBC. The game finished and through my ear 'cans' I heard the studio say: 'Well, that's it from Boundary Park.'

I was dashing back to do an MUTV appearance and it was at that moment that this guy passed and asked for my autograph. It was bloody freezing and I started scribbling away when another voice came down the line and asked me if I fancied being a manager. I thought it was idle banter and shouted, 'Never mind that. It's fucking freezing here. I need to go.' Rob Philips turned to me and said, 'We're still on air!' Oops. I was still live on air and I had filled the BBC Wales airwaves with the worst possible expletive. There wouldn't be a welcome in the hillside after that.

On the Monday morning I got the phone call I was dreading from the head of sport in London. He said, 'We don't condone swearing, even if it was cold.'

I immediately apologised and he added, 'OK, everyone makes mistakes. We're willing to give you one more chance.' And then he left me with the parting shot: 'To tell you the truth, I didn't realise how popular the show was. We have never had so many fucking complaints in our lives.'

I'd kept my job and the more my voice was heard the more work came in: *Soccer AM* and later Century Radio in Manchester alongside my good mates Gary Owen, Alan Kennedy and Graeme Sharp. MUTV appearances came thick and fast. Not bad, I thought, for a kid who was a dunce at school and had to write those letters to clubs asking for a trial by using a dictionary on my bedroom floor.

I'm as honest on the air as I was when I played the game. I tell it how it is. I don't beat around the bush and nor does Joey. We come from rough-arsed council estates. I'm still there, of course, but these days I have got windows in the frames.

Life's great again. And I thank God I have emerged through personal hells without losing my marbles or being locked up in an institution. I was always a prime candidate, though, for falling foul of the pressure that often threatened to blow my head apart.

Twenty-six

Pressure: eight letters that can lead to a multitude of problems. And for most people, just like myself, it can be kept hidden so easily under the surface before it finally rips you apart. For today's manager it's a massive, massive job to keep every one of his players in focus. And he doesn't know what's really going on in the minds of his men.

The fans don't, either. They see their heroes playing ninety minutes and then see photographs of them in the newspapers enjoying themselves at celebrity bashes or sunbathing and swimming in exotic locations. Happy on the outside – being eaten away on the inside. A manager might have an idea about one or two of his charges and will be able to react. But keeping an eye on an entire squad of twenty-eight-plus is a virtually impossible job. Like me, many will be able to hide their true feelings. And today the pressure is even more immense. You have to remember and appreciate that footballers come from different walks of life.

I came from a rough background and I was in no way ready or prepared for that big step up. It happened so fast in my case, going from little homely Wrexham to Manchester United, one of the biggest clubs in the world. I couldn't control anything that happened to me. The enormity of being transported from earth to somewhere on another planet had a devastating effect on me mentally. Other players experience their own hell.

I wasn't the first to buckle under the pressure. I won't be the last. In modern times we have had Paul Gascoigne and Tony Adams falling foul of drink. Paul Merson admitting to drugs. These big star names came out and revealed that they had hit booze or drugs because they couldn't handle the pressure in their particular chapters of life.

But the problem of self-inflicted abuse of the body and the mind has always been there. The difference is now it's fully recognised. It wasn't in my playing days. It would have been embarrassing for me to admit that I was feeling the pressure for the whole of my time wearing the famous red of United. People would have laughed, ridiculed me. Mocked me and told me to pull myself together. I couldn't.

I came from an era where you didn't like to admit anything like that. If you got knocked to the ground then you bloody well had to get back on your feet again. No one suspected, anyway. I was a broken man inside, but all observers could see was this little winger with a mop of black curly hair having the time of his life playing for the famous Man United.

My pressure was appearing in front of those fans. My pressure was getting and keeping my place in the team. My pressure was putting in the kind of performance those thousands expected every week. That was the pressure for me. They only saw Mickey Thomas the footballer. They didn't see me as a fragile human being who couldn't handle my footballing life.

They didn't understand the problems I was going through mentally. How could they when the mask never slipped outwardly? Back inside the Old Trafford dressing room I became adept at hiding my feelings. We would all sit around as a group, as a team. Different characters. Different mind sets. Some strong. Some lacking confidence. Some, like me, unable to cope with the pressure.

We all had our problems. Some were bigger than others. Many could handle theirs. I was one individual who just couldn't hack it in that particular phase of my often troubled life. Mentally I was distressed but no one knew. I kept myself to myself. I didn't confide in anyone.

Everyone assumed I was Mickey, the happy-go-lucky, cheeky chappie. A cocky little guy without a care in the world who loved his job. Far from it. I had so many demons in my head and I couldn't kick them out. It was literally doing my head in.

I had a good career at the time with United and played at the highest level at Old Trafford and other stages across the world. But I didn't really express myself at United as I did at other clubs. And I still regret that to this day. I felt it was too big for me. Although I played some fantastic games for United I always felt that I played well within myself. I was never able to show those fabulous fans the true Mickey Thomas. I couldn't be the person I wanted to be. I wanted to be me, but I became far too inhibited. I was trapped in a cruel world of self-doubt.

I recently saw one of those old classic games on Sky: Wales against Scotland. I murdered the old enemy. Made a mug of Scotland and nutmegged their centre back on the day, Gordon McQueen. Oh, and I scored two goals. That old TV pundit Jimmy Hill said in the studio, 'What about Mickey Thomas?' His fellow front man, former United great Lou Macari, agreed that I was a different player when I appeared for my country. They both felt I was more at home playing for Wales.

And they were dead right. I didn't get that warm glow of feeling at home when I was at United. I was invariably in the team, but it wasn't the real Mickey Thomas out there. I could have done better, much better. The pressure left me reaching all too many times for that wine bottle on the eve of home games in a desperate attempt to find the confidence that had deserted me.

The only thing I can say, hand on heart, is that I never turned to drugs. I don't think players in those days knew anything about them. I wouldn't have known where to get my hands on them even if I had wanted to. Taking drugs never crossed my mind.

I would never condone it, either, but there's a part of me that can understand the temptation for today's players. And I'm not just talking about established stars, here. The pressure of life on and off the field can lead a few down that dangerous path, including youngsters in the early stages of their careers.

Drink, I think, is still the biggest evil and destroyer of careers. Look at the case of Joey Barton who got into punch-ups at Manchester City and was sentenced after that early-morning brawl in Liverpool city centre while playing at Newcastle. That's a classic example of too much too soon, and in his case was nothing to do with pressure on the pitch. When you get the wealth of cash in your wallet like Joey you begin to think you are all-powerful, that you are better than anyone else.

The more I got the more I spent. I couldn't control my finances. I wasn't educated enough to handle all those wages, bonuses, appearance money and flash cars. Maybe today's footballers get a lot more in the way of advice on money matters. Not many care to listen.

Personally, I just couldn't imagine being a nineteen- or twenty-year-old getting a million pounds a year.

When you get that ridiculous amount of money at such a young age it's very hard to stay on a straight road. You get a lot of hangers-on, too – people who call you their friend but don't really know you. There are so many packs of hyenas out there ready to pick the monetary flesh off the bones of an unsuspecting young star. Too many are out there to take advantage of a footballer, past and present.

That's why I'm now putting myself forward for what many would consider a highly unlikely role: a counsellor. I think the PFA should employ me to go around clubs and talk to players. I have had the experience of being there and plummeting into every pitfall going. I have quite a track record.

Ex-players like myself, Merse and Adams should be recruited to help others after what we have all been through. We have had major problems and come out the other side, so who better to guide young players embarking on hopefully wonderful careers?

If my problems could have been identified at an early age it could have made a world of difference. Who knows? I could have stayed at Manchester United for a long time instead of running off to Everton.

You can see a definite pattern in the way some players react to being battered by their demons: George Best, Merse, Gazza and Adams. There's a catalogue of people whose careers have sometimes suffered after suffering similar problems. They have been well publicised.

What about the ones you haven't heard of yet? The stars going through the same nightmares but who are nowhere near ready to come out? They are probably too scared to come forward. I could help them through their personal minefield.

I'm a more professional person now and I never thought I would be able to confirm that bold statement. I have the experience, good and bad, of being a footballer and a human being surviving in this tough world of ours.

And I haven't even touched on that other career-wrecking vice – gambling. Secretly there will be a lot of young kids – and established players – making too-frequent trips to the bookies, betting on the Internet, gambling in casinos. There are so many outlets now for players to exploit their addiction.

I turned to gambling big time when I was young. Most of my money went in the casinos. I had to have a release, and playing the roulette wheel or dealing cards was mine. Like all footballers, I had too much free time. It was very difficult to chill out for so long every afternoon without gambling becoming a constant companion.

After training at United, I would get straight down to the bookies and do in all my wages on the horses. Later in life, the casino became my second home. I loved spending my money, and even in extreme gambling cases like mine you always think you are in control of your addiction.

You never are. There's only ever one winner. I've lost a fortune over the years. I often lost all I ever possessed – but then I could just go and make some more. I've never kept an accurate record of what I have blown. That wouldn't be my style, would it? Maybe it's £250,000. Maybe it's more like £500,000. Thinking back, that's probably nearer the mark. And I'm not proud to admit that. It was easy money. Easy to blow £10,000 on a spin of a roulette ball or the flick of a card. It's an addiction that began at United but it's one that has grabbed me more in my later years when I retired.

Most of the time it's boredom. More often than not it's a release of pressure. To many professional footballers money doesn't mean anything. Merse had a lot to contend with: drink, drugs and gambling. He had a full house. I will always remember him crying at that press conference when he came out and admitted his major addictions. It was a huge release for him because he had identified what was destroying his life. I applaud him for that.

I applaud Tony Adams, too, for fighting back from the brink and re-establishing a fabulous career, which saw him play a major part in Portsmouth's FA Cup victory over Cardiff. I have great admiration for such a true leader with Arsenal and England.

My advice to anyone heading for the slippery slope is that you have to stand back and address your problem. Talk to someone, unlike me in my days of hell. You might think you have your problems under control but if you don't seek help, your addiction – whether it's drink, drugs or gambling – will rapidly spiral out of control.

Don't be afraid to confide in someone: a friend, a member of your family or your boss. Or someone like me. That way, you might have half a chance to beat your addiction.

I could have free-fallen into a black hole of despair and self-pity when I came out of prison, turned to my addiction to help me get through the grim times. But I decided to keep my focus and get myself back on my own two feet. I borrowed some weights and trained for four or five hours a day on my own. I concentrated my mind on working hard on my body. I kept my often too wayward brain in check and rejected thoughts of going off the rails. I had to look after myself. No one else does in this life. Now there's not one part of me that believes I will crack and go downhill.

Drink will never be a problem again. I don't touch a drop now and have only fallen off the wagon once in the past four years. It was on my fifty-third birthday when I was invited out by a millionaire friend of mine, Mike Walsh. We went to Wings Restaurant in Manchester – and I nearly grew some. I drank so much champagne I was totally out of my head. I was ill and not for the first time I thought I was going to die.

I knew then that drink doesn't suit me. It was another

reality check. So, yes, I don't drink any more. I'm a tea man. I just love a nice cuppa, anytime, anywhere. Call me Mickey Tea from now on.

Twenty-seven

Moscow, and Manchester United's nail-biting Champions League win over another of my old clubs, Chelsea, was one of the most exhilarating nights of my life. Although I've been around the football circuit as a player for so many years, that rainy night in Russia takes some beating.

I'm just proud that I was part of it, thanks to my media role. There it was, the gleaming European Cup – the trophy that all the top clubs on the continent set out to win – plonked on one of the seats of the homebound plane less than twenty-four hours after the penalty shoot-out win over devastated Chelsea.

Just talking to the players – and the fact that they knew me and accepted my role – gave me a terrific buzz. But the everlasting impression was the way Manchester United – the manager Sir Alex Ferguson, the players and all the staff – looks upon itself as one great big happy family. That takes some doing in an era where big business and big money seem to rule.

Everyone was shaking hands, embracing and chatting at Moscow airport the day after one of the greatest triumphs in the club's rich history. The United players are very approachable, very down-to-earth lads, despite all the success which could easily turn people's heads.

I was on a high just being around the event – a fitting finale to a fantastic season for United. Yes, I count myself a lucky man being able to sample the atmosphere. When I was a player, this club had been too big for me and I couldn't stand the pressure, but now I was lapping it up, on the back of what today's talented United squad had achieved.

I had been part of the commentary team for the radio station I work for – and I confess that the penalty shoot-out really got to me. In fact, it affected me so much that I had to turn my back on it on occasions. I so desperately wanted United to win, even though I had probably played the best football of my career with Chelsea. It's just that the majority of my media work has revolved around United.

When Cristiano Ronaldo had his penalty saved I really thought that United were going to lose. I felt for them because they had been the best team in Europe over the season and deserved the ultimate reward in the shape of the Champions League trophy. Even so, I felt for John Terry when he blew the penalty that would have made Chelsea Champions of Europe. I have a lot of respect for him and my heart went out to the Chelsea skipper. If anyone was to miss I wish it had been Didier Drogba, who got sent off.

I would have been delighted if Drogba had missed a penalty because in my opinion, before he was red-carded, he hadn't played well. Here is a six-foot-plus fantastic football specimen, all muscle, going to ground as if he had been shot. Even the Chelsea fans had grown tired of his tricks. We never had players likd that in the seventies and eighties. If we had have done they wouldn't have lasted long.

Drogba wasn't the best advert for the Premier League but in the end he lost out big style. Chelsea did well to reach the final but it's United who play the more pleasing style of football and that wins through for me every time.

It was so apt that Sir Bobby Charlton led the team up to collect their medals at the end of the game, fifty years after the Munich air disaster. The script had obviously been written by the gods. It was also pleasing that there had been no trouble between the two sets of fans in or outside the ground. In fact, there was plenty of good humour and banter going around. All the aggression that sometimes gives the game a bad name was thankfully absent.

There was a fantastic banner held aloft by some Chelsea fans: 'Scouse Free Zone.' Brilliant! It's an event that will live long in the memory, not just for me but for everybody who made the long and expensive trip.

By the time the United players were ready to board their plane the next day you would have thought some of the excitement would have abated. No way! Albert the kitman was dancing about all over the place, whilst the players were laughing, joking and patiently signing autographs. Just looking at the excitement in the eyes of players like Ronaldo, Owen Hargreaves and Ryan Giggs showed you what the game is all about. A lot is talked about the financial rewards that football brings but strip it all away and the thrill of winning the big prizes overrides everything. Most are just down-to-earth lads who love playing football.

I spoke to Ryan and his mum and told them both that the season couldn't have ended any better. Ryan had scored the killer second goal in the win at Wigan which clinched the Premier League title and had scored the vital final penalty in the Champions League success. Oh, and he had also just overhauled Sir Bobby's all-time United appearance record.

It couldn't have happened to a nicer bloke. But knowing Ryan he won't want it to end there. He will be after even more medals this season. That night in Moscow just confirmed the narrow dividing line between success or failure, something Chelsea had to come to terms with.

United go from strength to strength and much of that is down to the gaffer, Sir Alex Ferguson. He has always been good to me – will shake my hand and have a few words. It's amazing what he has achieved. He is the head of this incredible family, the godfather if you like. Witnessing at first hand the excitement and the pride in him tells you a lot about the man. There's no way he is going to walk away from the team he has built. A lot of hard work has gone into his latest Old Trafford model. He has spoken about what can happen once you have retired. There have been countless examples of people retiring and going off to meet their maker. Fergie will be thinking, That's not going to be me.

Especially when he has got talent like Ronaldo and Wayne Rooney around him. There was all the talk of Cristiano going to Real Madrid in the summer but there was never any need for him to move away from Old Trafford. He's playing in the best league in the world, he scored forty-two goals last season. I know from bitter experience that the grass is not always greener on the other side. I've done too many runners, but here is a man who should stay put.

He looks contented among the United family and he was quick to join in the singing as the plane came into land at Manchester airport. A steward started a rendition of 'Glory, Glory, Man United' and everyone joined in. There I was – who once would never go near a plane because of my fear of flying – loving every minute and not even with a drop of alcohol for some Dutch courage as I've given up the booze.

Looking around at the players I realised just how young they are and how much more there is to come. Ronaldo, Rooney and Carlos Tevez should be here for some time yet. Wayne, for instance, came to United to win trophies. He is doing that. He is a very humble lad, a credit to his profession. He has also got married in the summer, something the manager always approves of because it usually means the lads become more settled. Anyway, not many people walk out on Manchester United – except me, of course!

There's just one cloud hanging over United: what to do when Ferguson eventually calls it a day. It has taken a long time for someone to come in and match the great Sir Matt Busby. In the end, that person was Sir Alex. The club will be left with a huge decision when he calls time on the most successful reign in the club's history. I know I would have loved to have played for him. He is someone who immediately commands respect. Maybe under him things would have been different for me at Old Trafford.

Who knows? But one thing is for certain: I've enjoyed being just a small part of that happy United family, and Moscow in May will never be forgotten.

Twenty-eight

Unbelieveable – there couldn't have been a bigger contrast in my emotions at the end of an eventful season.

Manchester United had given me one of the greatest nights of my life but my first football love, Wrexham, were down and out. They were relegated from the Football League for the first time in their history. I still can't believe that they are now members of the Blue Square Premier League – how the mighty have fallen.

All those memories of the great European nights, the promotion into football's second tier, the darlings of North Wales. Now I believe they are fighting for their very existence, not knowing whether they will ever be able to renew old acquaintances in the Football League.

That is grim, believe me. A town that is used to being members of the ninety-two club élite is facing the stark reality that while they might have a splendid stadium, the football club is now amongst the paupers. What really annoys me is that the warning signs had been there for a number of years. They almost met this same fate the previous season but still the problems weren't addressed.

All right, they brought in Brian Little as manager, and he has plenty of experience. But the change didn't do any good, and to compound everything that has happened the best players – those who could have brought Wrexham straight back – have been allowed to leave. That is a crazy decision and one that may come back to haunt them.

Their drop out of the Football League has really hurt me and I know my big mate Joey Jones who is still part of the club is absolutely devastated. The night when it was confirmed that Wrexham could no longer preserve their league status was one of the saddest of my life.

That's what this game does to you. One minute you are ploughing the depths with your first club and the next you are experiencing the sheer nectar of being part of Manchester United's success.

But it's Wrexham's sad plight that is never far from my mind. It has been a real choker. To lose their league status is a nightmare for all concerned. That club has not only caused a few shocks in the past, it has also brought talented young players through. What's going to happen to that conveyer belt now?

This is the severe kick up the backside that I believe was always just around the corner for a club on the slide.

Now unless Wrexham can get their act together pretty swiftly, the whole affair could turn fatal. There might not be a Wrexham as we know it in a few years' time.

Look into the Blue Square Premier League and see the number of former League clubs stranded there. Some, like Scarborough, have gone to the wall. Halifax have flirted with the same danger. There is no guarantee that once you drop out of the Football League you are ever going to get back. It really is pitiful that Wrexham could now join that band of no-hopers.

The people I mostly feel sorry for are the fans. They have always stuck by Wrexham in big numbers. Now they face a huge challenge. Are they going to turn up for the likes of Northwich or Grays Athletic? Not exactly inspiring fixtures when you've had Arsenal and Liverpool come to the Racecourse Ground over the years. The supporters have definitely been let down badly. This has affected the whole community; it's been a real shocker. I saw them play on occasions in that last fateful season and they didn't look good enough. Too many of the players appeared to be more concerned with their personal image than with trying to help Wrexham escape the drop. I hated seeing this: players who obviously thought they were bigger than they were. Well, the message with relegation came over loud and clear: you weren't as good as you thought – not by a long way.

Poor old Joey, what an experience for him to bear. He is part of the furniture there – in fact, he's probably like an old settee! He has a great love for the club and he is hurting. It was a strange old season for Wales. Wrexham have departed into the non-league while Swansea have risen into the Coca-Cola Championship, while Cardiff City reached the FA Cup final at Wembley. But Wrexham's plight is so sad for North Wales. It's still hard to comprehend, even now. And I have so many happy memories: winning promotion into the second tier with a 7–1 thumping of Rotherham; those balmy European nights; that FA Cup win against Arsenal in which I scored. But that is now all in the past and I don't think the future looks too bright.

I've had so many clubs that my emotions are bound to be triggered by one of them at some time. The climax to last season was no different. West Brom are back in the Premier League. They are a real yo-yo club but hopefully they will be able to stay up, although as everyone knows it's going to be tough because of the huge gulf between the Premier League and the Championship. You have to admire them. They always seem to be able bounce back from relegation. For tenacity they take some beating.

They have been joined in the Premier League by Stoke. As you know, Stoke are close to my heart and the connections are still there to this day. I am really excited to think that the big teams will be visiting Stoke again. What a job the manager Tony Pulis has done. And from what I heard, some of the Stoke fans have been known to give him a hard time. One thing you can't argue with is his record.

My old chairman Peter Coates is back there too and good luck to him. Although I wasn't happy with the manner in which I was released the second time around, I believe it's good for Peter to be back at the helm. He loyally answered the call when the Icelandic owners decided to sell up. You could say they just melted away! Thank goodness they did because, like a number of foreign owners of football clubs, they weren't there really for the football. Stoke wasn't going anywhere fast under them and hopefully now they will be able to defy the odds and stay up.

You never know, Jasper and a few members of the 'Naughty Forties' might just have to come out of retirement with crews from the big clubs due at The Britannia Stadium! Stoke for me belong amongst the big boys. Long may it continue.

Then there are Leeds United. In the end, the fifteen-point deduction did for them. They still almost pulled it off with promotion into the Championship through the play-offs. Ah well, poor old Ken Bates – not exactly the most popular man in football. I felt sorry for Leeds because it seemed that no one has a good word to say about them. I wonder why that is? It seems the critics are always lining up to boot Ken Bates and the club. I thought it got a bit too much last season, always kicking them when they were down. I feel that starting on a level playing field this time around they will get promoted this time from League One – and without the need to go into the play-offs. There, I can't say better than that, Ken, my old pal!

Twenty-nine

Most people when they meet me now comment on how fit I look. It's something I take great pride in, even though my passion to keep my body in tip-top condition once came close to killing me!

Being in prime fitness has been instilled into me from a very young age. I have always had this natural fitness and, with that in mind, it's ridiculous to think that I had those heart problems at Everton and a check-up at Brighton where the doctor there told me he had never seen a bigger ticker.

I've always been proud of myself when it has come round to my fitness. It's something that has remained with me until the present day.

These days I'm always up early, usually around 6.30 or 6.45 a.m. and I have a methodical fitness regime – one which I never even think about skipping. Nothing stops me from my routine. I will do three hundred sit-ups at home in the morning, one hundred press-ups. I also have some weights in the front room, which I use every day. Most people would have them in the garage, but as I've said, I haven't got a garage!

An important part of staying fit is my dog, a Staffordshire terrier called Asbo! What else? I'm always taking him for long walks, so that helps keep me active as well.

After a life of continual exercise, I know I've got to keep on going down that route. Because once you stop the engine that's when you are in serious trouble. I make sure my engine is ticking over all the time. Look around you now and see how many people have let themselves go fitness-wise. I believe I have the right ingredients to keep myself fit. I love to be able to keep playing in football matches, most of them now for charity.

Believe me, it's nice waking up and opening the front door every morning. I still remember when it used to be opened for me – by a prison officer! Those horrible memories of being locked in a prison cell have never left me. That's another reason for loving every minute of being alone in the fresh air around my Colywn Bay home. Living right by the beach is absolutely brilliant. It doesn't get much better than that.

Every day I can go running on the beach – as long as the tide is out! Mainly, though, I do a lot of walking in the mountains behind my home. I am out most days for hours and hours. I go all over the area. It just gives you a fantastic buzz. I also make sure I eat the right things. It's

Special K for breakfast. I hardly eat any red meat these days, it's mainly fish, brown bread. I love my Chinese food and I'm a regular in Wings, a top Chinese restaurant in Manchester when I'm in the city.

You are only given one body so you have to look after it. I want to stay fit and keep on being involved in football in as many ways as possible. Even when you're part of the media, as I now am, it's important to keep your body in the best possible shape. Being supremely fit is good for the mind and keeps your brain sharper. Because of the episodes with my heart I have my blood pressure checked regularly. You can never be too careful, but so far so good.

But all this fitness lark almost sent me to meet my maker just a few years ago. I've got a massive scar on my bald head to prove it after a horrific accident – the sort that could only happen to me. One day I decided, as I had on many other occasions, to go for a run around the Great Orme, the mountain that dominates the Llandudno skyline. It's a run of around five and a half miles. For a run like that – one I take really seriously – I always put on my baseball cap so that people don't recognise me. I never want any distractions.

Anyway I was running along the road, enjoying myself, when I heard a car coming and just jumped onto the pavement to get out of the way. Bang! I ran straight into a low-lying sign, which I hadn't noticed. It was a horrendous collision. I can't remember to this day what the sign said – I doubt I noticed it when I went headlong into it. I joke now that it was probably emblazoned with the words: 'Mind Your Head!' It might have said 'Hospital This Way!' because that's where I would shortly be heading. It was no laughing matter, though, with me lying flat out on the ground in bloody agony. There was blood gushing everywhere. I can just about recall an elderly lady and a bloke coming to my rescue They asked me if I had been hit by the car that had just passed. No, I mumbled, I had run into that bloody sign. The ferocity of the blow obviously made them believe the car was the cause of my terrible wound. They had also heard the sickening thud of head hitting metal.

The lady took off her coat and placed it over me. One of them had obviously called for an ambulance because, thankfully, within a couple of minutes it arrived. Mind, the ambulance lads recognised me and asked me if I had been drinking. Here I am at death's door and my reputation was going before me. There wasn't any time for jokes, as they quickly discovered when they got me into the ambulance.

One of the medics actually gasped when he took off my baseball cap and saw the deep bloody cut. I started to panic. They were saying that my hands were going cold. I knew what that meant. I was in serious trouble. I honestly thought I was going to die. My mind was working overtime. I kept thinking that my dad had died of a brain haemorrhage. Was that about to happen to me? They were sticking needles into me and talking about taking me to Walton Hospital, Liverpool, which specialises in serious head injuries. They decided there wasn't time for that – I was going to the local Llandudno hospital instead. I was truly panicking by this stage, with all sorts of images flashing though my brain. One of them was of the fourteen-year-old son of the couple who had looked after me in digs when I first went to Wrexham. He had died after falling off his bike and banging his head. There was also the memory of a skateboarder who had recently been killed after coming off his skateboard and striking his head. It wasn't looking too good for me.

I was thinking that my addiction to fitness was going to end up killing me. Many addictions do get you in the end. But trying to keep fit? There's no greater irony than that, surely? My sense of humour had for once deserted me. I was just desperate to live. Once in hospital, no one could believe what had happened and the extent of the injury. I ended up having ten great big staples in my head to stop the bleeding. I can still feel them going in to this day. The only consolation was that I was surrounded by some pretty nurses. One of them commented on how brave I was being. Believe me, I felt like screaming and crying because of the pain but there was no way I was going to do that in front of them. The whole experience was absolutely horrendous. I was really shitting myself. For all I know, I probably already had. I could easily have died but thankfully after spending a couple of days in hospital I went on to make a full recovery.

Word of my bizarre accident soon got out and Tim Lovejoy even got me on Sky's *Soccer AM*. He asked me what time it happened. I told him two o'clock. He asked whether that was two in the morning. See, I can never get away from my past when I did used to be up to no good in the early hours. This had been no joke. At least I successfully sued the local council for positioning a sign too low and in a dangerous place. I got £5,000 out of them and probably could have gone for more. They didn't even contest the claim. Anyone could have struck their head on it. It just happened to me – and at full pelt. Nothing much has stopped me in my tracks during an interesting life – a bloody Welsh sign did!

But it hasn't put me off. I still go running because being healthy is what it's all about. It keeps your mind active. There's no way I want to slow down. Another thing I'm proud of is that I'm the same weight as when I was playing. Yes, I'm still the same 10 stone 10 lb as I've always been. I do have a few eating vices though. I love a few chocolates, a few puddings. I did have a really sweet tooth but my dentist has got it now! But as long as you exercise there are no real problems in allowing yourself the odd naughty luxury. It's also being part of a super-fit family, with Aaron being a boxer and Jade a kick-boxer and footballer. I love bouncing up those steps in the press box at Old Trafford, proof that I feel great. I've also played with and against some of the press guys in charity and challenge games. I remember nut-megging Oliver Holt of the *Daily Mirror* in one match when I was representing the Welsh media against their English counterparts. After the game, Henry Winter of the *Daily Telegraph* who was on the England side, said he couldn't believe how old I was after seeing me run around on the pitch.

I want to keep on playing in those games for as long as I can. I have always said I am not bothered about the level at which I play, as long as I can still do my bit. I sometimes go for a run with either Aaron or Jade and that gives me a kick. It was nice that Lou Macari, a Manchester United great, recently told me that he hadn't seen anyone fitter for their age than me. Luckily, I've always been able to run the legs off most people. I don't want to stop. I have a passion for being fit and Stanley Matthews was still playing when he was sixty so there's still a bit to go for me yet.

Thirty

In football, success always came easily and readily to me. Shame I couldn't say the same about my love life. My marriage to Debbie ended bitterly but we still see each other. Debbie was too young when we married and I probably wasn't ready for such a commitment myself. I don't blame anyone for the break-up. And, as always, I look for a positive and find it in my two great kids, Aaron and Jade.

I always drilled it into them from growing up in our little council house that they had to stay strong, stand on their own two feet. And they had to do that sooner than they bargained for. Aaron was thirteen and Jade ten when I was sent to prison, and the way they handled that trauma in their life made me so proud.

I didn't want them to write to me in the nick. I didn't want to make a big issue out of the fact that I was in jail. I knew, and they did to, that I would be home after nine months behind bars. I could handle that short time in my life. And I expected them to handle it, too.

My mum Maureen was there for them in my absence. My sister Pauline and my brothers, Kevin and Phillip, were always around. And the kids knew that my mate Joey and his wife Janice were close at hand and would always keep an eye on them.

I was home more than the average prisoner anyway, so it wasn't as bad as it could have been for the family I left behind. Aaron and Jade didn't come to any harm. The Thomases wouldn't have let them. And now, as I look back on their young lives, I do so with so much pride. They've each gone their own way in life without any pressure from Dad – and they've not let me down.

I wanted Aaron to be a footballer. What dad doesn't? But I'm not going to argue with him after he chose to become a professional boxer. He's much bigger than me and he's got a longer reach.

Aaron toyed with the idea of being a footballer, though. There was a lot of pressure on him but I didn't want to push him too hard. I did take him to Barnsley once as a kid for some training and he enjoyed that. He definitely showed promise and had good ability. He was physically strong, naturally strong as a lad, but looking back I could see he would be more suited to fighting than football.

There were plenty of scraps on the street when he was growing up. Other kids picked on Aaron because he was my lad. You know what kids are like. He would get called names and only knew one way to react: he hit out. He was good with his fists, too.

So I took him to Ricky Hatton's training camp in Manchester for the experts to have a look at him. Ricky's trainer Billy Graham and the Hitman himself were impressed. Ricky said to me, 'Your son boxes like a pro. You can tell just by his sparring that he's got talent.'

Aaron was on his way and although he turned to boxing late in life – at the age of twenty-four – he quickly made a name for himself. He became Welsh Amateur Champion, which was a great achievement, and he later represented his country at the Olympics in Sydney.

When he turned pro, Aaron won his first three fights as a lightweight – and I will never forget the first fight at one of my favourite places, Stoke. You guessed it. The Naughty Forties came along in force to give my boy support. About three hundred Stoke fans were there in all. Jasper, Salty and the lads certainly got right behind Aaron.

The atmosphere was electric, the noise deafening. Or so I'm told. I can't stand watching Aaron fight. I get too nervous for him. I don't want him to get hurt, even though he is a tough lad and can handle himself. Instead, I stood outside the hall.

I paced outside on the pavement and just briefly popped back in to ask the guy on the door, the bouncer, how the fight was going.

'I don't know,' he said, 'but the lad in the black shorts is a real nutter.'

I thought: Oh no, he's going to get battered. And curiosity got the better of me.

I poked my head inside and the lad in black was my boy Aaron. He certainly looked mad and he stopped this guy called Martin Sweeney in the second round – knocked him out. Not that his first opponent could have won anyway. He had three hundred Stoke fans to contend with and if he had beaten Aaron he would have had to face the Naughty Forties. No contest.

His victory gave me as much delight as scoring a goal myself. And although I'm disappointed he didn't become a footballer like his dad, I'm pleased he's gone his own way in his sporting life. I also admire him for getting in the ring in the first place. I'd have done one of my famous runners if I had to climb in there. I'm not sure how far he wants to go in the game. That's up to Aaron. But he's back buzzing again after having a bit of a lay-off. He's a hungry lad again.

Aaron has my support. As does Jade, who plays for Liverpool Ladies as a striker. She's good and, like me, has played for Wales. Jade is sports mad and as well as playing her football she's also into kick-boxing. She's had two fights – and won them both by knockouts.

Now, I can watch her fight. I don't have any worries on that score. She reminds me very much of myself: aggressive. Jade is exactly like me except she's got long hair and she's far prettier than her bald-headed dad. She's got great skill at kick-boxing and football.

I took Jade with me once to a Masters Soccer tournament in Manchester when she was about nine. I let her mess around with me on the indoor pitch and my old playing mates stood around in amazement. There she was juggling the ball, keeping it up, and then hammering shots galore into the top corner. It did my heart good when I heard some of the lads say, 'That's Mickey's daughter.'

Jade's a gorgeous girl and I'm proud, too, that she has been signed up for a few modelling dates. Portfolios of photographs have been taken and she looks great. But I don't really want her to go down that glamour route. I know where it leads. I don't want my daughter to get her boobs out. She's still living at home with me so I can keep my beady eye on her. Aaron's at home, too. We're all still under one roof, talking endlessly about sport. Just the three of us.

There has been a wild rumour, though, that there could be four. A year ago a guy from the *Mirror* came knocking on my door in Colwyn Bay to ask if there was any truth in the story that I had a love child. It was a mistake. I haven't. I know I always joke that I have got a kid in Sweden, one in France. But I haven't. I wouldn't be able to hide a Mickey Thomas child, would I? I wouldn't do that anyway. I'm a soft-hearted person and I couldn't turn my back on anyone with my blood running through their veins.

I have had unbelievable things happen to me. But a love child isn't one of them. I've got enough hassle looking after myself. But although I believe I'm a little softie, I still have a strong personality.

I'm a great believer that because I have always been good to people I will always get something back in return. I have always been a very generous person, always helped others out. I have always given my money away. The trouble is I see everyone as my friend. That's been my biggest downfall in this crazy life of mine. I take everyone on board the good ship Thomas as my pal but there are a lot of people out there who don't have my principles.

I can say, though, that I have never let my family down. I have always been there for them all. I drill into my kids not to worry about what anyone else says as long as you have your family. Outside those four walls of our house in Colwyn Bay, the majority of people will talk about us anyway.

Often it's not nice, but I tell the kids not to worry about it as long as they have got their family behind them for support. My family have always supported me and I'm still the same person who walked out of the house that day when I joined Wrexham football club.

My sister Pauline has always been a rock for me. My brothers, too. Kevin could have made it in the game. He was a very talented footballer and people always said he was the best out of the three of us. A great midfield player. Phil went to West Ham for a couple of days but he couldn't handle it because he didn't like life in London. I don't know why but he walked out and fled straight back to Colwyn Bay.

Now who does that remind you of?

Thirty-one

One sad aspect of today's game is the lack of access that the fans have to their idols, the players, especially at the higher end. The rapport between those who pay to watch and those who are paid to play is at an all-time low and that can't be good for the future.

The majority of today's high-earning footballers are superstars, untouchable and unreachable. You see them in their Bentleys and Hummers with blacked-out windows. The only blacked-out windows I was ever associated with were those in the various police vans that I travelled in!

It would be impossible for anyone – myself included – to refuse the vast fortunes on offer today. It's human nature to try to do better for yourself, but surely not at the sacrifice of losing touch with the outside world and reality.

Being part of the media circus these days, it also pains me to see the growing gulf between many journalists and football people. I am lucky that I tend to be better received by most players because, after all, I've been one of them and have been around the block a few times. I remember as a player that most of us would have decent relationships with football reporters. We would have a drink with them, enjoy nights out, in the knowledge that if anything untoward went off it would never get into the newspapers. I know that given the chance the same thing could happen now. The trouble is I fear that all this will remain in the past.

Also, it appears that many of today's young players can't take criticism. I had a simple rule as a player: if you are prepared to receive praise then you also have to be able to put up with the brickbats. Of course, no one likes that side of it but you just can't cut off the media if that happens, which seems to be the order of the day right now.

I'm not the first person to ask where the game is heading. But I pose the question because football remains in my blood. It's my passion and I would hate to see it destroyed. I have to admit there are worrying signs surrounding the game's future.

There seems to be no limit to what a top player can earn. The word recession obviously doesn't equate with footballers' wages. There are ridiculous amounts on offer and for average players.

More money hasn't helped us at an international level, has it? Look at England. The biggest salaries in the world are being lavished on the stars of the Premier League but England had to watch as the rest of the continent was involved in Euro 2008. England is supposed to be a great footballing nation but it hasn't won anything of note since 1966.

I'm afraid young players reach the comfort zone far too quickly. It makes you wonder if and how they can maintain any hunger for the game. Then, of course, there are the distractions of being a footballing fat cat at such a young age. And few people are there to catch you if you fall. That's where former players like myself can come in useful. I have the experience of going down the wrong road in football. And, as I have said, I believe it would be beneficial if the PFA, for instance, utilised the experience that old players like myself have by sending us out to talk to players and warn them of the risks ahead. Believe me, football can become a dangerous land, it can become a wasteland, even for players who feel they are in paradise. That slope can be very slippery if you allow yourself to go anywhere near it.

A lot of people don't understand the psyche of the modern footballer, and why should they? They see players picking up great wads of money, being mollycoddled and doing something that they do on a Sunday mornings for fun. If it was only that simple. That's why I could be useful in passing on my knowledge.

Sadly, I can't see any budding Mickey Thomas out

there sitting painstakingly on his bedroom floor writing letter after letter to football clubs in the hope of getting a trial. I can't see many of them having the patience, and also there are so many distractions now. Football isn't the be all and end all as it was for most kids when I was growing up. There is, I feel, an unhealthy desire to become famous, as you can see from the success of all the television reality shows. But it's mainly for the wrong reasons. The biggest reason for joining the fame game is to share in the riches that naturally go hand in hand with stardom. Somewhere along the line respect goes out of the window.

When he was manager of Manchester City, the England coach Stuart Pearce asked a young player what would he rather have: an England cap or a Porsche. He was horrified when the player went for the car. I was with the former Aston Villa striker John Deehan when he was in conversation with some young Villa players. Knowing they were interested in tennis he asked them whether they were going to watch any forthcoming tournaments in this country. No, they replied, they were off to New York to watch a few balls being hit. Yes, it's a different world to the one I knew as a player.

OK, the top players have plenty of money at their disposal but sadly for some of them there is always a high-profile disaster lurking just around the corner. It's so easy to be led astray, to fall off the straight and narrow. Look at Paul Gascoigne's sad plight. There is nothing more certain than that there will be lots more Gazzas.

Maybe some players don't listen any more to what their managers tell them. I remember, even as someone who had his moments, that if John Neal, my manager at Wrexham and Chelsea, said something then I took notice. If it was a verbal clip around the ear I would take it. How difficult is it now to keep a young millionaire in check? A manager is more likely to risk being told where to go if he tries to tell off a top player. If you've got millions in the bank then there is very little that can threaten you.

Another disappointing departure from when I was at my peak is that few top players are willing to drop into the lower divisions to keep playing. One, they don't need the money: two, do they really care that much about the game? Many don't share my love of football, my passion for it. There are, I'm glad to say, some exceptions. Players like Ryan Giggs and Paul Scholes at Manchester United love every minute of playing. John Terry and Frank Lampard showed at Chelsea that they love their football.

I'm just glad to see that Giggsy has been busy taking his coaching badges. You want personalities like him and Scholesy staying in the game. They have so much to offer, with their experience and enthusiasm. Money isn't and never has been their god. They are as passionate now about football as the day they entered it. I can see Ryan going on to manage Wales, which would be a great thing for my country.

I'm also worried about the growing influence of foreign owners in the game. It was virtually unheard of in my day for someone from outside the area of the club – never mind from outside the British Isles – to be running it. Let's face it, these invaders from overseas aren't over here for the love of the game. They are hard-nosed business-men looking for a quick return from their investment.

I have to say now that the Glazers who own Manchester United have been good for the club. They are the exception, though, rather than the rule in this foreign invasion. They stay in the background and are supportive while he gets on with the most important issue of managing. I have also spoken to members of the Glazer family and their knowledge of football is very good. As far as I know, they haven't blocked Sir Alex in any of his plans.

If only some other managers in the Premier League were able to boast that. Some of the situations brought about by foreign ownership at other clubs have bordered on farce. Look at Liverpool with George Gillett and Tom Hicks. A club steeped in tradition reduced at times to a laughing stock because of the constant boardroom bickering. It hasn't been much better at Manchester City under Thaksin Shinawatra. At least the former Thai prime minister has got one decision right: he has appointed Mark Hughes as manager.

Add the fact that the playing staff is overhauled virtually every season, and you can see why many fans can't identify with their clubs any more. Everyone seems to just be passing through these days, whether they are the owners, the manager or the players. That can't be good for football, which always needs continuity.

As far as players are concerned, testimonials are becoming a thing of the past. How many stay loyal to one club for ten years or more these days? Players move from club to club so quickly that their names should be written on the back of their shirts in dissolvable ink!

The game is going down a dangerous road. You see smaller clubs trying to keep up with the pace of the big spenders – and with shocking consequences. Look, for instance, at Gretna in the Scottish League. In what should have been a fairytale, they overstretched them- selves, spent one season in the Scottish Premier League but are no more. It's a fate that could befall a number of clubs north and south of the border in the coming years. It has already nearly claimed the lives of Leeds United and Luton Town. Leeds, especially, have known some heady days but they almost crippled themselves with bulging debts. That's a lesson for all clubs.

Fans are starting to vote with their feet. Season ticket sales were down at many clubs during the summer. The supporters I speak to are fed up with a perceived lack of loyalty from players, in addition to the sky-high wages. They have become brassed off with the constant upheaval and fed up with ever-changing kick-off times to suit TV schedules. Football has gone haywire.

There's big money but there also has to be big concerns right now. I know that if I was playing today I would be among the big wage-earners. Am I jealous? Not one bit. It would only have meant me giving away more than I used to. After all, I didn't do badly. I think my top wage was about £800 a week at Leeds which was pretty good at that time. I don't resent today's wages but I don't want the game to be destroyed.

Not enough of today's players are taking the step into coaching or management when they reach their thirties. For me it means there is a dearth of young talented managers coming through. There are exceptions, but they are few and far between. Paul Ince looks a good bet to go right to the top, especially now he is at Blackburn Rovers. He went down the old path of starting in the lower leagues with Macclesfield and MK Dons. He has also played under some top managers, so he certainly has the right pedigree. Mark Hughes, on the other hand, flung himself in at the deep end by starting his management days in charge of Wales. He has done well for himself.

It's important to surround yourself with the right staff because management these days is too tough for one individual to dominate it. I believe, certainly in the Premier League, that you've got to be able to operate in the transfer market with considerable funds. You are there with the big hitters and you've got to be able to compete.

I've always admired someone like Neil Warnock, who has been prepared to mix it with the big boys, more often than not fighting against the odds and rival bosses. He isn't the most popular person in the game – in fact, he gets up more than a few people's noses, which is great. I love that. Neil will have a go, though, and you can't knock that.

The pity is that many of the bigger clubs seem afraid to take a chance on a Neil Warnock. They would rather hand out the job to a Johnny Foreigner or one of the many failures of the game. It seems that managerial merry-go-round of failure exists in this country. You get sacked and then you are taken on by one of your rivals. It doesn't happen in any other business. No wonder some outsiders look in at football in amazement.

Why aren't the up-and-coming managers of the lower leagues given an opportunity by the big boys? There's Gary Johnson. He did a tremendous job at Yeovil and has repeated the feat at Bristol City. But he is never linked with a top Premier League side.

I also accept that there are many trigger-happy Premier League chairmen out there who don't give you a real chance once you're in the job. Getting rid of a manager after one or two years is a recipe for disaster. Mind, as I've said, the failures are well rewarded and usually bounce back into another job quickly enough.

While there are an abundance of foreign managers here it doesn't seem to be a two-way street. Few of our managers are given the opportunity to stretch themselves abroad, which is a pity. When I was playing, going to the USA helped me as a person. I'm certain it would be the same for some of our managers. Or maybe they are too lazy. Now that's something no one can accuse me of being!

Thirty-two

Throughout my career I played with some of the world's greatest and I feel honoured to now make my selection of who would get a start in Mickey Thomas's All Star Eleven. I thought of naming my greatest-ever side from stars of my era, but I prefer to pick from a much smaller, more élite squad. So I am selecting from the lads I played alongside, who made a close-up impression on me for very different reasons.

I have studied long and hard, sifted through players from my various clubs and those who played in the same red shirt of my country, Wales. And now I make no apologies for revealing my final line-up, which would undoubtedly have won any Champions League final before going on to beat anyone in the world with a true Brit side of undisputed winners. So here goes . . .

GOALKEEPER: Neville Southall. Without doubt, big Nev was the best goalkeeper in the world in his time. If he had been English he would have had even more recognition. I've spoken in glowing terms earlier about Nev, but for me he was the greatest.

RIGHT BACK: Mickey Evans. You might be surprised at this choice when I played with a glut of good defenders. But Mickey was a strong lad. Reliable. In our early days together at Wrexham he reminded me so much of Joey. Committed. He never put in a bad performance. Honest and dependable. A consistent performer week in, week out, who should have gone on to bigger and better things if Lady Luck had shined on him. A real team player, which is what I always liked about him.

CENTRE BACK: Gareth Davies. The captain of Wrexham at one time, who could have gone on to make a great name for himself at Manchester United. United's Tommy Cavanagh was driving to the training ground at the Cliff one day when he told me just how close they came to signing him. United went to watch him in one particular game and were going to sign Gareth at the final whistle. But sadly he got injured and they never pursued it after that. That's how tragic this game can be. Gareth was a great player. Very consistent. He made a marvellous captain and played in one of the greatest ever Wrexham sides.

CENTRE BACK: Martin Buchan. A perfectionist. Martin would always wear a suit and tie, even to training. Yes, a very smart man. And a truly inspirational captain for Manchester United. A leader of men. Martin led by example. A proper players' player and a very, very good defender. I definitely thought he would have gone on to become a top manager but obviously that didn't happen for him. As a captain he was one of the first players you went to for advice and who you looked up to on the pitch. He did everything in the right way. I remember when I left Old Trafford, Martin sent me a lovely big cheque. He told me it was mine by right. I was entitled to it: a bonus from the players' pool, which he was in charge of. I didn't know anything about the money and he could have kept it for the rest of the lads. But no, he wanted me to have it. Martin's only downside was his guitar playing and his choice of music on the team bus. He was one of the good guys you meet in life and never forget. Fantastic.

LEFT BACK: Joey Jones. Who else? Without doubt the most amazing character on and off the pitch. I will always remember one game for Chelsea against Sheffield Wednesday when the ball was bouncing six yards out and Wednesday were certs to score. But Joey put his body on the line and flung himself at the shot to block it. By the look of his face now he must have put his mush in the way of a few blockbusters, too. You talk about great players being strikers, the goalscorers, who get all the credit. But he deserves so much praise for an honest and brave career in the game. People hated playing against him. He was physically strong. Tough. A man's man. Long before Becks, he filled his body with tattoos when he was a kid at Wrexham. That's the way he is. Mad. You could rely on him in every game, though. He could certainly spray a winger any time he wanted to. Another 110 per cent man. I played in a trial at Colwyn Bay as a kid and I scored a hat trick. Joey got a hat trick, too – he put three players in hospital. He's one of the first in my team. Mind you, he'd kill me if I left him out.

RIGHT MIDFIELD: Steve Coppell. The most intelligent player I have ever met. He was very unlucky with injuries and was forced to finish with a very bad knee injury. He was so quick and a great crosser of the ball. But he could do his fair share of tracking back, which I liked about him. You get great players going forward but not many great players track back. He certainly did that. Steve went from grammar school to the University of Liverpool where he got a degree in economic history. Some cruel jibes now say it must have been a degree in depression. I got mine in shagging. He was a great bloke. I went to his house once after a game and it was bloody cold. He didn't have any heating on. So he gave me this lovely England top to keep me warm. 'Put this on,' he said. 'And remember, Mickey, I want to get it back.' He never did. I admired Steve in more ways than one. Everyone said I had two lungs. He had three legs by the way – make your own assessment of that one.

CENTRAL MIDFIELD: Mark Hughes. The Legend. People use that expression freely but Mark's a proper legend in the game. He's done everything in football here and at Barcelona and Bayern Munich. A great goalscorer. He saved one of the greatest for Wales against Spain at Wrexham. A top player. Strong and physical and he had great presence about him. Mark was quiet off the pitch but he was a monster on it. A big man. In the dressing room he didn't have to say much. His ability out there said it all. And he could look after himself, Old Thunderthighs. He put himself about and you couldn't mess with him. You wouldn't dare. Not many people argued on the pitch with Mark. He gave everyone a tough game and always showed real commitment.

CENTRAL MIDFIELD: Sammy McIlroy. The last of the Busby Babes. Sammy had great footballing skills and amazing ability. He possessed such a wonderful touch. To play alongside someone like him was a great honour for me. He had everything. He had so much ability and scored one of the great goals in the 1979 FA Cup against Arsenal, which will always be remembered even if United lost. The way he dribbled into the box. Wow. I'm still excited by the goal even now. A great guy and a good manager as he's proving now.

LEFT MIDFIELD: Pat Nevin. Another intelligent player. How come I've surrounded myself with two wide men who are such clever people when I'm such a thickie? Pat, too, had everything. He wasn't the biggest of builds, but he had great vision. A superb awareness of where players were. He could flick the ball anywhere and he became such a cult hero at Chelsea and quite rightly so.

He went to Everton but didn't have the same impact as he did at Stamford Bridge. Pat was a player who could win you games and create the incisive opening. A fabulous player.

STRIKER: Kerry Dixon. He didn't just score at Chelsea, he hit the net wherever he went. He had the knack of being in the right place at the right time. In my spell at Stamford Bridge he was a phenomenal goalscorer. He played for England and got goals for his country, too. He was my kind of player. Tough as old boots. Another of my players who could look after himself. I was lucky to have played with some great centre forwards but as well as being prolific he was bloody awkward to play against. Another giant of a guy who could definitely mix it in the toughest of company. I love centre forwards like him who don't take any prisoners. People will always talk about flair. He had that but he could stick the ball in the back of the net for fun. You don't get better than Kerry.

STRIKER: Ian Rush. The best goalscorer there's ever been for Wales. All the talk was always about Gary Lineker but for club and country, Rushie never got the universal recognition he deserved or warranted. To me he was the perfect striker. Amazing. I remember sitting in the back of a car with him and I asked him how he could stick the ball in the net the way he did. His answer was typical Rushie. He just shrugged his shoulders and said, 'I don't know.' He had that electric speed in and

KICK-UPS, HICCUPS, LOCK-UPS: THE AUTOBIOGRAPHY

around the box and he worked his bollocks off for the team. Worked so hard at closing people down. And he scored so many goals in his wonderful career. He was always destined to become one of the best players of all time for Wales and he didn't disappoint. His record speaks for itself.

I'm just glad I didn't pick myself in this All Star team. I wouldn't have even put myself on the bench. I would just be happy sitting in the stands watching my marvellous side. So who would be on the touchline as manager? That's another easy one. The only candidate would be my old gaffer at Wrexham and Chelsea, John Neal, because he had that belief in me and he would have belief in my side, too.

I have had some great managers in my life and John's appointment is no disrespect to the others: Arthur Cox, Dave Sexton, John Giles and co.

Thirty-three

Now my life has come full circle and after my poor upbringing in monetary terms, the early days at Wrexham, a tour of clubs in England and America, and jail, as Elton John would say: I'm still standing. And I've got a great job, too. I might not have been able to hack it completely playing for Manchester United but I certainly don't have any problems following them around the world for my media commitments.

I feel more relaxed reporting on United than I ever did when I was wearing the famous Red Devils shirt. There is obviously not the same pressure on me looking in from the outside than when I was on the inside. And I don't mean the slammer.

To this day, though, I still feel honoured and privileged that I played for such a great club. I have been in those United players' shoes but it's their time now. And, believe it or not, I am not envious one little bit.

It's a different world now, a footballing world that has

changed for the worse. From the days of watching football on a tiny black-and-white TV screen as a kid to when I was actually playing is a light year away from life as we know it now. The modern man is living on a planet infested by agents. It's the 'what am I going to get' syndrome. Planet Hollywood.

Sadly, the innocent years, the fun years, have disappeared. They have been submerged in a bottomless pit of money and greed. The problem is youngsters coming into the game have it all too easy. And I really hope I'm not talking like a grumpy old man here.

There is no such thing as a proper apprenticeship, where kids with stars in their eyes have to undergo the time-trodden chores of cleaning boots and sweeping out the dressing rooms. Health and safety anoraks have long put paid to that grounding in football life. And that is absolutely pathetic.

I remember when I signed for Leeds United, Gary McAllister came up and told me that he used to clean my boots at Old Trafford. It was just something you were expected to do but more importantly you were proud to do it, thinking that maybe someone would repay the compliment when you had made it in the game.

The time has come, I believe, to seriously consider knocking down the wall built between the players of today and their supporters. Dismantle it brick by brick. I know we're never going to go back to the days when football greats of the day boarded the ordinary No 53 bus with their boots tied round their necks. But somehow a little access has to be restored.

I always think that on my many visits to Premier League grounds around the country. Get to the stadium early and you will see the same scenario: players arriving in their limos, parking up and being escorted by security men from the VIP area into the executive entrance. Have they lost the common touch, or what?

Earlier last season I was at Portsmouth. It was after the game against Manchester United and I was standing near the touchline and having a chat with Harry Redknapp and Joe Jordan, my former United team-mate. Both old school. A few minutes later I saw England star Sol Campbell and some of the Portsmouth players walking along the side of the pitch ready to go home. Each one of them had a steward escorting them off the premises. Bloody hell. What the hell is going on?

When I played my football, I had a great rapport with the fans. That might have contributed to my downfall, I don't know. But today's protection surrounding the players is ridiculous.

Talking of protection, I still can't stop wondering how my career would have taken a different path if Sir Alex Ferguson had been in charge at Manchester United when I arrived from Wrexham with more dreams than Joseph had in his technicolour coat. Sir Alex has ruled with a rod of iron and a warm arm of compassion around the shoulder at the same time. He's guided his players well. Look at how he came to deal with Ryan Giggs in his formative years, shielding him from the media when he could have fallen foul of the champagne world of Playboy Land.

It's not just knowing how to deal with players on the pitch that is important to Ferguson. It's what happens to his troops away from Old Trafford that occupies his mind just as much, if not more. He has the uncanny knack of seeing a problem developing early. He identifies it and deals with it.

I am certain if he had been around in my Old Trafford days I would have undergone a real football education or whatever I needed. You won't see his like at Old Trafford again. Here he is, more than twenty-one years in charge and still going strong, with retirement currently a couple of years away.

I'm just pleased that he knows who I am. I can still picture in my mind's eye playing for Wales the night that Scotland manager and former Celtic great Jock Stein died. Ferguson was alongside Stein that night.

And it always gives me a thrill that players like Giggsy and Paul Scholes show me respect. Just them saying hello to me gives me a huge buzz. It's the same with other well-known players who I am lucky enough to meet all those years after I played on the same stage as they do now.

I was down at Chelsea's training ground one day and I asked John Terry for a signed shirt. He told me that I could definitely have one of his – as long as I could give him one of mine. Now that was some gesture on his part. You can't get much better than that: the Chelsea captain wanting my shirt.

Then, even more amazing, José Mourinho, who was the manager at the time, saw me and came straight over. I couldn't believe it when this great giant of the game shook my hand – and then bowed. He said that he had been told that I had been a great player at Chelsea.

I said, 'Thanks, Mr Mourinho.' And immediately he told me to call him José. He even invited me to sit down and have some dinner. That made this little five-foot-plus guy feel ten feet tall.

A number of people have been good to me in the game. When I was right down on my arse and needed some signed shirts to raise some money, I remember first ringing Glenn Hoddle who was then the England manager. He wasn't in and someone told me that he would ring me back. I thought there was no way that was going to happen. I just hoped it would because I was so desperate for cash. Well, Glenn left a message on my sister's phone, which I'd used because I didn't have one.

'Mickey, Glenn Hoddle here,' he said. 'Anything I can do for you, no problem.'

So I phoned him back and he got me a signed England shirt.

Graeme Souness was top class as well. We'd had those spats I have described down the years but he got me some autographed shirts as well. He told me that he had always respected me as a player and that if I needed anything else then I shouldn't be afraid to ask.

Peter Reid, who was manager of Sunderland in my many hours of need, told me the same. That I shouldn't be embarrassed about ringing anyone because I had done more than most in the game.

Those three phone calls put me back on the road to recovery. From being on my backside not wanting to speak to anyone, I was even able to arrange that testimonial at Wrexham. That £38,000 I made wasn't a fortune but it helped me slowly get back on my feet. I'll never forget the generosity from football legends and the ordinary fans for as long as I draw breath.

I've been through some shit in this troubled life of mine but now Media Mickey is full of beans again. I'm happy with my lot – and delighted to be rubbing shoulders with the game's greats.

Like Sir Bobby Charlton. He had a good joke with me when I asked for his autograph. And Giggsy wrote in his own autobiography that I was his footballing hero. That was amazing because I have always been in awe of Ryan. And it was so strange when I interviewed him once for the BBC.

I hadn't ever met him before and I was nervous. But at the same time I heard that he was nervous about meeting me. I did the interview and he gave me his football shirt. He used to watch me from the terraces and now it's me watching him. And what a fabulous player he still is.

The father figure that is Sir Alex has certainly kept his 'son's' feet on the ground. But no one around Old Trafford can ever relax or assume that they are a permanent fixture at the club. There have been too many times in Fergie's reign where his boot has landed firmly on a superstar's bum and launched him out of the doors.

Ferguson can be ruthless when needed – or when he felt the time was right to pull rank. Look at what happened to the likes of Norman Whiteside, Bryan Robson and Paul McGrath. They all went when Sir Alex thought it was right to call time on all three who were big drinking buddies.

I agreed with Fergie when he dismantled the David Beckham circus tent, which had pitched up at Old Trafford. That was a show the United boss would never allow to take centre stage. Sir Alex felt that Becks' showman life, with all that Posh Spice hype, had to end.

That's why Ferguson has remained at the top. He's not afraid to make big decisions. Paul Ince will tell you all about the time when he was pushed onto a plane to Milan in a sudden exit, the speed of which even shocked the guv'nor.

I thought at the time that the Beckham business was getting too big for anyone's golden boots. No one individual is ever bigger than Manchester United. And judging by the trophies Ferguson has collected since Beckham left, the manager has once again been proved right.

One thing is for sure, after last December's party antics in a Manchester city-centre hotel, there won't be any more Christmas bashes at United for the players. What happened last time around – with an allegation of rape – really hurt Fergie.

Since that adverse publicity, Ferguson has ensured headlines are concentrated on what happens on the field. And right now there is no better or bigger club to cover, media-wise. Any club could win the Premier League for the next ten years but the same euphoria that surrounds United wouldn't even get near to touching any other team.

Not that my media life safeguards me from some of the crazy incidents that have gripped my own playing career. It has been known for yours truly to go tumbling down the steps of a plane at Manchester airport – without a drink touching my lips.

My fall from grace came when we were ready to fly to a Champions League game in Hungary. I was climbing the steps to the cabin when I tripped and went hurtling back down again.

The United doctor examined me and told me I had cracked a rib and couldn't possibly fly. I can still recall Paul Scholes and John O'Shea looking at me in disbelief. They should have seen some of the scrapes I got into as a player.

Anyway, off I went, with a police escort taking me off the runway at high speed. Those flashing blue lights on top of the cop car certainly brought back memories of my past involvement with the men in blue.

For the first time in my life I wasn't running away from an aircraft, desperate to go home to Colwyn Bay because I was scared shitless of take-off and landing. I wasn't that impressed with all those hours stuck at 40,000 feet, come to think of it.

I was embarrassed when I missed so many flights over the years because of my fear. Now, thanks to personalities like Dennis Bergkamp, the major problem I had about flying has been identified.

Gone are the days of horror when I would turn up at the airport sweating with fear – and turn myself around again and head back to Wales. Strangely, I'm more comfortable about flying now, even though I can't say I love it.

It's the steps that are the problem!